# LONG SHOT

## LEAH CHURCH

To all those who have been told
that your dreams are a long shot ...

Energion Publications
Cantonment, Florida
2023

Copyright © 2023, Leah Church. All Rights Reserved

Scripture quotations are from The ESV® Bible (The Holy Bible, English Standard Version®), © 2001 by Crossway, a publishing ministry of Good News Publishers. Used by permission. All rights reserved."

Cover Image by Jeffrey Camarati and used by permission of the University of North Carolina

ISBN: 978-1-63199-873-7
eISBN: 978-1-63199-874-4

Library of Congress Control Number: 2023950507

Energion Publications
1241 Conference Rd
Cantonment, Florida 32533

pubs@energion.com
energion.com

To my family,
who has been there for me since day one …
a constant source of love, prayers, and support.
Thank you for demonstrating Jesus in all that you do
and for your examples in my life.

I love you!

# TABLE OF CONTENTS

Preface: Desires of the Heart ..................................................... 1

| | | |
|---|---|---|
| 1 | The Early Years | 5 |
| 2 | "Bleed Carolina Blue" | 9 |
| 3 | Balancing life | 15 |
| 4 | The Hoop Shoot | 19 |
| 5 | The Hoop Shoot … Part II | 25 |
| 6 | My Siblings | 29 |
| 7 | On the Horizon | 33 |
| 8 | The Shadow | 37 |
| 9 | Recovery and Recognition | 43 |
| 10 | The Preparation | 47 |
| 11 | Another Answered Prayer | 51 |
| 12 | The Sting of Reality | 59 |
| 13 | Moving On | 63 |
| 14 | Seeing Red | 67 |
| 15 | A Dream Come True | 71 |
| 16 | Celebration | 77 |
| 17 | The Journey Begins | 81 |
| 18 | Not All Fun and Games | 87 |
| 19 | My Support System | 93 |
| 20 | Overcomer | 97 |
| 21 | Highs and Lows | 101 |
| 22 | Standing Alone | 105 |
| 23 | The Mountaintop | 109 |
| 24 | Repping My Country and My Faith | 115 |
| 25 | Disappointments | 121 |
| 26 | Unforgettable! | 125 |

| | | |
|---|---|---|
| 27 | The Battle Line | 135 |
| 28 | The Time has Come | 143 |
| | Afterword: Long Shot | 151 |
| | The Last Chapter … For Now | 155 |

# PREFACE

# DESIRES OF THE HEART

*Delight yourself in the Lord
and he will give you the desires of your heart.*
— Psalm 37:4

> "Down three points to No. 15 Duke with four seconds left in regulation, North Carolina women's basketball head coach Sylvia Hatchell drew up a play. Who did Hatchell trust to shoot with the game on the line? It wasn't Paris Kea, a preseason All-ACC Team pick who finished the game with 36 points and five made threes. It wasn't Jamie Cherry, the senior leader known for her clutch late-game shooting. It was Leah Church, a first-year averaging 3.1 points a game."
> (Daily Tar Heel newspaper,
> *Take me to Church,* January 22, 2018)

It would take a long shot. But first things first...

A little 7-year-old girl would write, "I want to play for the Carolina girls when I grow up. I have been practicing basketball and running laps around my house. I am trying to keep in shape if I ever make it to the Carolina girls." These are the words found in my homeschool newspaper, *The Family Journal.* Don't most children aspire to be famous, a pro, or celebrity? They have dreams and hopes of reaching lofty heights and being known. My dream would begin before I could even write those tell-tale words. The writing was "on the wall," as they say, but it often would look blurred and sometimes even erased.

Most kids have a bent towards playing with balls when they are just a baby and "ball" is often a child's first word. So, my parents didn't give it too much thought when I was constantly playing and throwing balls, at a young age. However, at about age three they say there was just something different. Ball is all I wanted to do. It started with our church league, Upward Basketball. My dad was a pastor at Millers Creek Baptist Church and the head coordinator for our county's Upward League. Naturally, I thought that I would be on a team and playing basketball that season. Unfortunately, Upward had an age requirement of 5-years-old. My little heart was broken, as I saw my older sister, Taylor, playing ball, yet I was not allowed. To smooth things over, my dad got me a jersey, whereby the smallest size still dragged the floor. Dad even let me participate in the "evaluations" used to balance the team's talent level. This included things such as dribbling around cones, passing, and shooting on a lowered goal. People said that I scored higher on the evaluation, as a 3-year-old, than some of the older kids who participated. Maybe that's when my parents knew that basketball just might be my thing.

The next year of Upward rolled around and an exception was given for me to play up a year. Boy, was I happy! I got out my Carolina Tar Heel arm bands, put one on each arm, and donned my Carolina headband. These were the thick retro ones, not the thinner head ties that are a bit more stylish these days. Looking back at pictures, I laugh at myself, as I really thought I was the "stuff." I played with reckless abandon, too. In Upward Basketball there was a rule for the younger kids that you can't pick up your man on defense until the offense crosses the half-court line. Well, I decided that I would be waiting for whoever crossed that line with the basketball. As soon as they stepped over, I would strip them of the ball and score a lay-up. Each week, the coaches gave out stars for things such as defense, offense, sportsmanship, Christlike-ness, effort, etc. I guess it is no surprise that almost every week, I got the offense award. The Christlike-ness award went to the kid that didn't pressure the ball! Even at that young age, all I wanted to do was shoot and score. Whether that was good or bad, shooting was a passion and a love that I must have had from birth.

During those early years, my dad would take me to the church's gym almost every afternoon and let me shoot on the lowered 8-foot goal. I always wanted to go and shoot with my big sis on the 10-foot, but Dad wanted me to learn technique first. So I just shot, shot, shot, and shot. To this day, no one has ever taught me how to shoot. Shooting was a God-given talent that the Lord used to shape my life and my path. This was just the beginning of a long, yet miraculous, journey in which there have been ups and downs, victories and failures, tears and laughter, doubts and fears, and moments I wanted to give up on my dream. It is a story of a little girl from Purlear, a small town in Wilkes County, NC. It is a story of a little girl who was determined to play basketball at the University of North Carolina despite being barely 5'8", homeschooled, and sub-par on the athleticism spectrum. It's a story about a girl who relied on her faith in Jesus, found her strength in her family, and made up her mind to never let the "naysayers" stop her from pursuing her dreams. This is the story of a little girl with a big dream who served a big God. Thanks for joining me as I share my journey!

# Chapter 1

# The Early Years

*Behold, children are a heritage from the Lord …*
— Psalm 127:3a

I was born in Wilkes County, NC and have lived in the small town of Purlear, NC since I was three-years-old. Most people have no clue of the location of this little town of just over 2,000 people, so I usually just say, "I live thirty minutes down the mountain from Boone." Many tend to know where this college town is located, as it is known for Appalachian State football, beautiful fall leaves, and ski slopes.

I was raised in a Christian family, where my dad was a pastor and my mom stayed home with me and my older sister, Taylor. Taylor is three years and three months older than me and, although my polar opposite, she is my best friend. People are often flabbergasted when we say we never fought. Well, there was that one time that we got in an argument and Mom made us put 50 cents in a jar every time, thereafter, that we said something mean to one another. That solved the problem quickly, because I'm tight with my money. My dad says I squeak when I walk. So, once I realized that the dumb thing we were mad at each other about (of which I don't remember) was costing me money, I got over it. Anyway, when people asked how we always got along so well, Mom attributed it to reinforcing how fortunate we were to have each other. She would tell us that out of all the sisters and girls in the world, the Lord chose us for each other to be best friends. We were constantly told how blessed we were to have one another, and fighting was never an option or allowed. I think that this mindset helped us, but it also made a difference that Taylor was the kindest person on the face of the planet and did everything and anything for me. I was the strong-willed kid who pushed the boundaries and quite often got a well-deserved spanking. Taylor was the kid who got one spanking ... literally **one** spanking her whole life. That lone moment occurred when Taylor disobeyed and got out of her toddler bed. Mom claims that I had a bit of a rebellious streak in me, was hard-headed, and strong-willed, but she always knew that my personality would serve me well as I got older. Reeling it in at a younger age was sometimes the painful part. I am grateful for the discipline and love that my mom and dad showed me while growing up. It helped mold me into who I am today.

Our parents felt called to homeschool me and Taylor from the very beginning. They believed that they should live out Deuteronomy 6:7 which says, "You shall teach them (the Lord's laws/ways) diligently to your children, and shall talk of them when you sit in your house, and when you walk by the way, and when you lie down, and when you rise." They felt that the only way for them to live this out was by homeschooling us. I am thankful they were obedient to God's calling, as it was one of the greatest blessings of my life. I was able to spend time with my mom and sister, who are now my best friends. I was protected from outside influences and was taught the ways of the Lord. I hear so many sad stories about the bullying that takes place in some school settings and the negative effects it can have on children. Although homeschooling was a sacrifice for my parents, they were intent on protecting me and Taylor. My mom had a master's degree in education and was teaching first grade in a public school when Taylor was born and made the decision to give up her career to stay home and teach her girls. At that time, my dad was a high school baseball coach and physical education teacher. The thought of moving to only one salary was daunting, but they trusted the Lord with it.

There were occasions when money was tight and one time, we didn't have enough money to get groceries. It was almost pay day, but that summer evening, we didn't have any food for supper. However, Taylor had gone to Vacation Bible School earlier that week, and the church workers had given out Burger King Happy Meal cards. She was given four cards. Mom says that we ate happy meals that evening, and Dad got paid the next day. Since they took that step of faith, the Lord always provided and made a way. He seems to do that when you walk in obedience.

I grew up living beside my cousins, Katy and Kandace, who were also homeschooled. Katy was about the age of Taylor and Kandace was my age. Many afternoons were spent playing at the creek, in the playhouse, or in their above-ground pool. Looking back, I am so grateful I had a childhood that was void of technology and social media. Instead, life consisted of the outdoors, our imaginations, and physical activity.

The four of us were a motley crew. Katy, the oldest, was the ringleader of the group, Taylor, the reasonable, rule follower, Kandace, the head strong, charismatic one, and I was the tomboy, who was into everything. There are so many stories I could tell. One day our moms told us not to get wet, in the creek. But four kids, under the age of ten, have short memories. One thing led to another, and we were all sopping wet, from head to toe. We ran to our playhouse in the backyard and took off all our wet clothes and laid them on the playhouse porch to dry. We were hoping the clothes would dry before we had to go back inside, to face our moms. Obviously, my mom saw that there were clothes laid out all over the playhouse and came out to see what was going on. She opened the door and found all four of us naked and huddled inside. I think because we were such a hilarious sight, we avoided getting in trouble that day. Then, there was the time that Katy convinced me to get in the creek on a snow sled. "It will float just like a boat," she said. Of course, it didn't, and I sunk. I was soaked to the bone on that cool fall day and so mad at Katy. On another occasion, Taylor claimed to have seen a snake in the creek and we ran (screaming at the top of our lungs) all the way up the hill to my house. To this day, we are still unsure whether it was a real snake-sighting or a figment of her imagination.

Katy was the drama leader and had us perform plays growing up. I was always the "boy" and played parts like "Linus," in our Charlie Brown Christmas play. We would charge our grandparents for admission to come see our shows and take up their cell phones so as not to disturb the production. Once the lights were dimmed and we passed out our brochure, it was all business. Man, our family members were good sports. There were many memories that I will hold onto forever and I truly believe those experiences were an essential foundation in my life.

# Chapter 2

# "Bleed Carolina Blue"

*And this is the confidence that we have toward him, that if we ask anything according to his will he hears us.*
— 1 John 5:14

During my childhood years and in addition to basketball, I also played softball and soccer. I weeded out soccer rather quickly but stuck with softball for several years. I was almost better in softball than I was in basketball. I made the all-star team every year and won more game balls than I had places to put them. I played for as long as I could in coach-pitch, but when fast-pitch rolled around, I made the decision to stick with just basketball. I have heard many people say that it's better to be a multi-sport athlete. I would say, "To each their own." I don't know that I would have been as successful a basketball player if I had played multiple sports. Plus, I truly loved the game, and I didn't have a desire to play anything else. I lived and breathed basketball.

I don't necessarily know what started this intense love of the game. Neither of my parents played basketball. Mom was a cheer leader and ran track in high school and my dad played football and baseball. However, my paw-paw played basketball in college and so did my uncle (on my mom's side). Looking back, I think that seeing UNC men's basketball win a national championship in 2005 sparked a love for UNC and the game of basketball. My entire family are die-hard Carolina fans and I had no choice but to love the Tar Heels. I had just turned seven when they were playing for the national championship in '05. I didn't own a UNC shirt, just yet. I remember going to Belk, the day of the championship, and Mom buying me a Carolina blue t-shirt to wear that night, when we watched the game on TV. After that win, I was obsessed with the Tar Heels. I could tell you anything about Raymond Felton and Sean May. I could tell you preseason predictions, names of recruits, and all the same information about Duke, as well. I had to know everything about the archrivals, right? I had a Carolina birthday party that year and everyone was required to wear Tar Heel gear, whether they were a UNC fan or not. I started building my Carolina wardrobe and pretty much all I ever wore was a UNC jersey and shorts. However, and much to my dismay, I had to dress up for Sunday church and forgo my Carolina attire. I changed my pink-painted room to Carolina blue and decked it out with a Tar Heel bed spread, pillows, and sheets and hung every UNC women's and men's basketball poster that I owned.

As some may know, tickets to a men's basketball game in the Dean E. Smith Center do not come cheap. It was a bit out of our price range, so when Mom heard that before their first game in the NCAA tourney, the team would be having an open practice in Greensboro, she knew this was my chance to see them live for the first time. We decided to make it a homeschool field trip and made the trek to see the Tar Heels practice. I was in awe! There were my heroes standing right in front of me. I'll never forget that day.

It wasn't long after this that we started attending the Women's UNC basketball games. Those were the days of the Carolina legend, Ivory Latta. Watching the Heels play in Carmichael Arena created a dream in my little heart. I committed to one day playing on that court in front of all those people ... no matter what it took! Until then, I did everything I could to be around UNC basketball. My parents made it happen.

It was a 2-hour and 15-minute ride home from the women's game, so we spent the night in Chapel Hill. At the game the night before, I noticed that there were ball kids for the team. To me, this was an exciting job! How great to be able to sit behind the goal and wipe up sweat after a player fell? I determined that I just had to be one of those kids. So, we waltzed into the women's basketball offices in Carmichael arena that morning. Dad, Mom, Taylor, my grandparents, and I entered the office and asked whom we needed to speak to sign up to be a ball kid. We were directed to Jane High, Head Coach Sylvia Hatchell's personal assistant. Not only did Mrs. Jane sign me up for a game that season, but she allowed us to go and shoot on Carmichael's basketball goals. Of course, I had brought my basketball with me … just in case. It was surreal to have the chance to shoot and play on the court where Michael Jordan played. I was in love with all the Tar Heel blue and Jordan logos, not to mention the championship banners and retired jerseys. It truly was Tar Heel heaven!

I was seven years old when I found out about Sylvia Hatchell's North Carolina basketball camps. The camp information stated that a child must be eight to register, but because my July birthday was close to the camp dates, they allowed me to participate.

Each year, I would save up some of my birthday and Christmas money to go to camp, during the summers. That first year, dear friends also helped us attend camp and as time went on several people would support me, financially, and come alongside my dream. My family, even my maw-maw and paw-paw went with me, to camp. They would bring bag chairs and go around to each gym. We would listen to Coach Hatchell proclaim, "We want you to love Carolina. We want you to bleed Carolina blue."

One year, my dad met another dad of a camper who was gym-hopping like my parents. His daughter and I were in the same group and he was carrying his bag chair around, too. My dad had just launched into full-time missionary evangelism that summer and as a faith-based ministry, he would start raising monthly support when he returned home from Chapel Hill. This man and my dad ended up having a conversation and shared about their lives. We would soon learn that he and his sister owned a credit card processing company in Texas and had a heart for missions. He suggested Dad and our family meet his sister when they visited Charlotte. We did and Dad was able to share his vision for our ministry, Craig Church Ministries. They began prayerfully and financially supporting us and to this day, they are our biggest supporters. Talk about a pre-ordained, God-sent meeting on the side of a basketball court! It's amazing how the Lord orchestrates ours steps and lives.

It is an understatement to say Carolina camp was the highlight of each year! I remember hardly being able to sleep the nights leading up to it. The campers had sessions at Carmichael and the Dean E. Smith Center. To me, the greatest thing ever was playing on those historic courts and in those arenas. I even got to tour the women's locker room and sit in a locker. Oh, how I wanted it to be MY locker with my name on it. "One day," I told myself.

I attended camp for years and developed relationships with many of the coaches and staff. The first year I attended camp, Coach Tracey Williams-Johnson, the director of recruiting, did a presentation on what coaches look for in players and how to get recruited. In my "autograph notebook" (the one I carried everywhere in case I ran into a player) I wrote down each of her 20 bullet points and took everything she said to heart. I remember, to this day, Coach Tracey saying, "You never get a second chance to make a first impression." After she spoke, my mom and I went and introduced ourselves to her. Mom told Coach Tracey that I was homeschooled and asked if it would be an issue for me in recruiting. She assured us (as only Coach Tracey could) that when and if that time came, homeschooling would not be a concern. Granted, that bridge would not be crossed for over ten years, but to a wide-eyed young girl, those words were reassuring. Little did I know, that was the beginning of a very important relationship.

Each subsequent year, I would speak to everyone I could and eventually, I became a familiar face. I bought Coach Hatchell's book *The Complete Guide to Coaching Girls' Basketball*. I read the whole book which was full of drills and coaching strategies and brought it to camp the next year for Coach Hatchell to sign. I was on a break in Woolen gymnasium, (UNC's non-air-conditioned gym, built in the late 1930's) when I saw Coach Hatchell walking around. Mom had kept my autograph book with her in case I got a chance to get her autograph. The moment finally came, and I was so excited! Coach Hatchell was very gracious and made one little girl's day.

I prepared so hard for camp each year. I would wake up early to go run laps around my grandparents' house, past my aunt's and uncle's home, and back to my house. As they said in the old days, "It was up hill both ways!" Too, the middle of summer is hot in the foothills of NC and humidity is often oppressive. Nevertheless, I would replicate camp drills and the one-on-one competition and practice my strategy. I was going to be the best I could be, in front of the Carolina staff and coaches! During my early years, I would move up a couple of age brackets to more competitive groups. Later, the girls got taller, bigger, and faster than me. I still worked and worked and gave it my all, but I started seeing that this dream of mine wasn't going to be so easy, after all. I soon realized that these hundreds of girls, at camp, wanted a scholarship to play basketball at the university of North Carolina … just like me.

# Chapter 3
# Balancing Life

*For everything there is a season,
and a time for every matter under heaven....*
— Ecclesiastes 3:1

Once I turned eight, I started playing AAU basketball, for the Wilkes County Diamonds. They were based out of Elkin, NC so we drove 45 minutes, one way, to practice. Weekends were filled with 5-plus games, 5 a.m. wakeup calls, and packed snacks. Growing up, we never allowed basketball to cause us to miss Sunday morning church service. Oftentimes, my dad would hold a service inside the gym's hallways and teams and parents would come. Sometimes the tournament director would even pause games for people to attend service on the main court. I learned to play the guitar when I was four and I put it to good use at a young age. By no means was I a professional, but I knew enough chords to play and sing a worship song before my dad preached. I was decked out in my full uniform, braided hair, knee-high socks and Nike slides, singing, "Here I Am To Worship," to all who came out. I learned that Jesus was always first and to be made the priority. Very early on, my parents taught me Matthew 6:33, "But seek first the kingdom of God and his righteousness and all these things will be added to you."

Around that same time, I struggled with feet/heel problems. The doctors said that my growth plates were separated, and it would take time for them to grow together. It hurt to walk, much less to run and play 5 to 6 games each weekend. My dad would take athletic tape and wrap my heel in heel-locks to try and secure the growth plates to manage my pain. It worked some, but the pain continued for several months, and it was tough for me to keep on playing. Thankfully, I grew enough to mesh the plates together and get rid of the heel pain. This wouldn't be the only time I would have to deal with something physical interfering with my basketball.

I continued playing for the Diamonds for several years, but my coaches and team changed, and I was forced to find somewhere else to play. There were not many local teams in Wilkes County, so I played for the Charlotte Warriors, located in Gastonia. The gym was almost a 2-hour drive from our house. Practices were on Sunday afternoons, so my parents, Taylor, and I would go to the early service at church, grab a quick bite to eat, and hit the road. Practice lasted up to 3 hours, then we would make the trip back home and get ready to start another week. Talk about some sacrifice on my family's part! We made a commitment, however, that whatever we did, we were going to do it as a family. That way, we wouldn't miss out on life together and we would have shared experiences and memories.

My dad was called into evangelism in 2007, which meant that he traveled all over the United States and the world preaching. Like we did with basketball, our whole family would often go with him. Many times, I would play my guitar and my mom, sister, and I would sing before Dad preached. We went to so many places, but one of my favorites was Brazil. Some of our Brazilian friends taught me, "Here I Am To Worship," in Portuguese and gave me a guitar to borrow and play. (Yes, that was my signature song, back in the day!) For me, going on a mission trip at such a young age was a needed experience. You learn early on how blessed you are, how good you really have it, and that life doesn't revolve around you. My childhood consisted of traveling to different places and hearing Dad preach. Between revivals, conferences, and interim positions, we've been to more churches than I can count. Because Taylor and I were homeschooled, we had the flexibility to travel and were fortunate to go to many places.

The Christmas of 2006, I made the decision to save up all my money to buy an in-ground basketball goal. I went to Dick's Sporting Goods and looked at every hoop they had and finally decided that I had found the one. It was a Goliath brand goal, had a 42" backboard, a padded goal post, and an adjustable height crank. It was the most beautiful thing I had ever laid eyes on! However, there was an issue … it cost over $600. Now $600, today, may not seem that insurmountable, but for a young, 8-year-old, it's a fortune. It didn't matter though, because I was determined to save up all my Christmas and birthday money. My parents went ahead and loaned me the money, with the understanding that I would pay them back, until it was all paid off. I think I ended up paying about $400 and then (like the good parents they are) they covered the rest of the cost. To top it off, my dad and I painted a Carolina blue half-court on our concrete driveway. It was the perfect finishing touch. Even after many hours of wear and tear, that painted court is still there and the Goliath basketball goal still stands today. It goes without saying that it was a rather good investment.

# Chapter 4
# The Hoop Shoot

*... but we rejoice in our sufferings,
knowing that suffering produces endurance,
and endurance produces character, and character produces hope.*
— Romans 5:3-4

Deep breath. Two dribbles. Elbow in. Release and follow through. If I hit these free throws, my name would be forever inscribed in the Naismith Basketball Hall of Fame in Springfield, Massachusetts. You may be saying, "Wait!" "What?" "How?" Let me introduce you to the Elks National Hoop Shoot, a free throw competition for kids ages 8 to 13. Nationally, every year, the winners of each category (a total of six kids) have their names inscribed in the Basketball Hall of Fame. According to the Elks National Foundation, over 3 million kids participate, annually. A local school in Wilkes County would hold the beginning stages of the competition. Because I was homeschooled, I didn't know anything about it until my maw-maw (who worked at the Board of Education) told me. Of course, I loved the idea of competing in this free-throw contest! I was always up for a challenge and something competitive.

In the Hoop Shoot, the first step in advancement is for a person to win from your school. For me, that was rather easy since Heaven's Treasure Academy only had two students, me and my sister and she didn't compete. Next, you had to win out of your county, then district, state, region (Maryland-Delaware-Washington, DC, North Carolina, Virginia, West Virginia) and finally, if you won your region, you advanced to the nationals. The National Hoop Shoot experience included an all-inclusive trip for the participant and their parents. Airfare, food, and a stay at the Sheraton Hotel in downtown Springfield, Massachusetts was paid for by the Elks Foundation. Also included was a trip and tour of the Naismith Basketball Hall of Fame and a banquet honoring the participants and champions. It was a chance of a lifetime and would be a dream if I ever made it to nationals.

The Hoop Shoot free throw contest had a very strategic and specific design. One Elk Lodge member rebounded, and one handed the participant the ball. There were official scorekeepers lined up on the side of the court and each participant drew a number for the order of shooting. When it was a participant's turn, she was allowed up to 5 practice free throws and then shot 10 free-throws that counted towards her score. After shooting 10, the person sat back down and waited for the others to shoot their shots. Once the participant's next turn came back around, she shot 15 free-throws that once again counted toward her score. All in all, it was the best of 25 free throws that advanced. If there was a tie, the person shot the best of 5 until someone won.

I was 10 years old when I signed up to compete and would be competing in the 10/11-year-old age group. I started practicing every single day. My dad would rebound for me at our local high school gym, and it became our everyday routine. I would shoot hundreds of free throws and replicate a contest. I shot 10 free throws and then would go sit at half-court for ten minutes. I envisioned the other girls shooting and then after I had been sitting a while, I would shoot my last 15. I consistently hit 24-25/25 in practice.

The county competition came early one Saturday morning. Of course, I chose to wear my favorite UNC jersey and rep my Heels. Fifteen plus girls were shooting for the spot in our local competition. I had never been in a situation or environment quite like the Hoop Shoot. It is an interesting environment because it is completely silent. There is no clapping, talking, or movement allowed. It is just you, the ball, and the rebounder, yet the stands are packed. Despite some butterflies deep in the pit of my stomach and a good dose of nerves, I advanced easily hitting 23/25 free throws.

The district competition was held two weeks later, at Lenoir Ryne University. The competition was much stiffer, as I was going up against a girl who had advanced to nationals the year before. Nonetheless, I advanced. Winning districts just gave me that much more confidence.

Up next was state and if I won it, I would travel to Maryland to compete in the regionals. I cruised through the state competition and was officially the best female free throw shooter (for my age) in the state of North Carolina! I received a custom NC sweat suit (in the color of none other than Carolina blue) to wear to regionals, as I represented the Tar Heel state. The Elks National Foundation paid for our gas up to Maryland as well as our hotel room and meals. I really thought I was something getting an all-expense paid trip and an opportunity to shoot to advance to the National Hoop Shoot. I was so confident this was my year. My family and friends had no doubt I would advance and win. I mean, I very rarely missed a free throw during my practice sessions, and I had easily advanced through the state competition. You might as well book my plane ticket to Massachusetts.

The competition, in Maryland, started with a ceremony where each state representative was announced while carrying their state flag. The participants then had a few minutes to warm-up before the official competition. I saw my competitors and thought, "I've got this." My turn rolled around, and I missed 2 out of my first 10. I was a little disheartened but knew I could hit 15 straight, my next turn. However, much to my dismay, I absolutely blew it! The moment got too big, and I psyched myself out. I suddenly forgot how to shoot. I would short-arm it. I would hold the ball and over-think every shot. I was missing free throws! This couldn't be happening because I never miss like this! I ended up hitting 17/25. I didn't advance, I didn't get to go on an all-expense paid trip to Massachusetts. I failed myself, my family, my state, and my hometown. Most importantly, I wouldn't get my name inscribed in the Basketball Hall of Fame. Devastated doesn't even come close to describing how I felt. I cried nonstop. I didn't talk the whole drive home from Maryland. Nothing about how I acted could categorize me as a "good loser." I felt that I was a failure, and no one could tell me differently. I really didn't understand why God wouldn't let me win. I always tried to honor Him, and I practiced harder than anyone else possibly could. I deserved to win! But did I really? Was there a purpose in me losing? Looking back, I realize that I learned lessons much more valuable than if I had won. I matured so much in that defeat. I learned that just because I do all the right things, my desired outcome is not always guaranteed. Nevertheless, that doesn't mean God doesn't love me or that I should stop doing the right things. It just means that His plans and purposes are different than mine.

> "For my thoughts are not your thoughts, neither are your ways my ways, declares the Lord. For as the heavens are higher than the earth, so are my ways higher than your ways and my thoughts than your thoughts." (Isaiah 55:8-9)

Oftentimes, in the moments of defeat or adversity, we can't see the good or the positives. It may take years to look back and see how God used that in our lives. During a crisis, it is difficult to remember that all things work together for them who love God and are called according to His purpose (Romans 8:28). But I can say that God has had a plan and will for my life, in everything He has allowed. You may be thinking, "Leah, that was just a free throw competition." You are correct. But, I'm a competitor. I don't like losing in anything, to anyone, anywhere. I don't care if it's a game of UNO, I will go all out to beat you. Too, I'm a perfectionist. Sometimes that serves me well and sometimes it drives me crazy. In the case of the Hoop Shoot, it served me well. Why? Because I had a choice. I could not participate in the next year's competition and be sure I would never again experience that horrible feeling of defeat, shame, and failure **or** I could not be satisfied until I got it right. What did "right" look like? For me, it would be doing my very best, not putting that immense pressure on myself, and not letting defeat control and paralyze me if I lost again. I guess you know what I chose. Yeah, the second option. I remembered the saying, "If at first you don't succeed, try, try again."

# Chapter 5

# The Hoop Shoot ... Part II

*For God gave us a spirit not of fear
but of power and love and self-control.
— 2 Timothy 1:7*

Fast forward a year. I'm at a gym in Frederick, Maryland, carrying the North Carolina state flag and wearing my Tar Heel blue sweat suit. Except now, it's a size bigger and the girl wearing it is a few inches taller. I was back in the regionals of the Hoop Shoot, back in the same gym where my dreams came crashing down a year earlier, and back with the same opportunity to punch my ticket to Massachusetts, for a chance to get my name inscribed in the Naismith Basketball Hall of Fame. I was ready and had prepared as much mentally, for this moment, as I had physically. I had made it a routine to quote Philippians 4:13 during my competitions and the times that I felt overly anxious ... which was quite often. I was at peace with myself, whether I would win or lose, but, boy, how I wanted to win and redeem last year.

I shot one of my best rounds ever during the Hoop Shoot, hitting 23/25 free throws. This was great except for the fact that another girl also hit 23/25, meaning we would go to a shoot-off. She would shoot 5 free-throws and then I would shoot 5. She hit all 5. Now, I couldn't miss one or it was over, and she would advance. I was literally shaking. As I write this, I have a clutch in the pit in my stomach because I remember how it felt. I couldn't let my mind wander to all the what-ifs, or I would lose my composure and choke. With God's help, I hit all 5 of my shots. Whew! I had survived and we had to shoot another round. She hit all 5, again. I didn't know if my nerves could take any more. I just had to hit the first one, as that is always the hardest. I hit it and the next 4. On to the third shoot-off. Finally, she missed one, which meant if I made all 5, I would advance to nationals. When I saw my chance, I took it! I made all 5 of my free-throws and was named the regional champ. I ran up the bleachers to my parents and sister and we all cried tears of joy. Just the year before, I had run up the bleachers to my family and cried tears of sadness and defeat. I had experienced the agony of defeat and now I was experiencing the thrill of victory. I was so grateful the Lord gave me the strength and steadiness to shoot. It truly was Him. I had trusted Him with it and left it in His hands, instead of trying to do it all on my own. God saw fit to allow me to advance and I was overjoyed. Book the ticket! I was headed to Massachusetts!

    I had become somewhat of a hometown "hero." All the local newspapers had interviewed me, and I even made the front page of the Wilkes Journal Patriot. For a small-town girl, that's big time. I was in the Winston-Salem journal and WXII News 12 had come to my AAU game for some game footage and an interview. I had an out-pouring of support from my county, as well as the entire state. I felt proud to represent Wilkes County, North Carolina, but also, homeschoolers. It was believed that I was the first homeschooler to come out of the state/region, since the existence of the Hoop Shoot.

    The next month quickly arrived and although the cost of attending the National Hoop Shoot competition was covered for me and my parents, we purchased a plane ticket for Taylor to attend. We arrived in Springfield the day before the national competition. Once we arrived at the Sheraton Hotel, our family went straight to registration. All the national championship trophies were lined up for the participants and parents to view. I took a picture with my age group's trophy, just in case I didn't get another opportunity to look at it. It was more than half my size and I thought it was the most beautiful thing I'd ever laid eyes on! The first night in Springfield, all the participants and their families went to an old gym that was within walking distance of our hotel. It was ancient! It reminded me of the old gym in the movie, *Hoosiers*. Because there were so many of us, each participant only had about 5-10 minutes to shoot. Afterwards, we toured the Naismith Basketball Hall of Fame and was able to see the plaque where all the previous winners' names were inscribed. I was praying that after tomorrow my name would be there.

Saturday arrived and it was time for the competition to begin. Beforehand, there was a big ceremony announcing each participant, along with all the other hoopla. It was like a miniature Olympic opening ceremony. There was music and we were all holding flags and marching around the court. If I wasn't already hyped up, I was now. Unfortunately, since I was in the second age group, we had to sit through the 8/9-year-old competition. There were twelve competitors in each group, so it didn't exactly go by quickly. I just sat there and prayed, visualizing myself at the line. Right before I got up to shoot, I had my mom pray with me as I did before every game or competition.

It was finally my turn. I took off my warm-up jacket, revealing my Carolina jersey, and took my warm-up shots. I had drawn fifth in the order of shooting. It would be a wait! I hit 9/10 in my first round. I was frustrated but couldn't let it get to my head. My shot didn't feel quite "on." Was it the nerves? Was the immense pressure getting to me? I got up to shoot my last 15 and ended up only hitting 21/25. That wasn't going to be enough ... not at the nationals. I held the lead, but there were still three more girls that had a chance. The best shooter was up last. I sat down and waited. I teared up as I prayed for a miracle.

My score stood through the next two. The last girl would have to miss four to tie and five for me to win. After watching her shoot her first ten, I honestly didn't think that could happen. Today, this girl plays for Oklahoma and is the NCAA's active career leader in three-point percentage. But when God has a purpose, the improbable can happen and His plan prevail. She missed five. I won! I sat in my chair sobbing. Joy and relief overwhelmed me, and I looked in the stands to see that my family was crying, too. They gave me thumbs up and I felt such a sense of accomplishment. Losing the year before made it that much sweeter!

Honestly, even to this day, that competition was the most nerve-wracking experience of my life. My parents say they were sick to their stomachs. We can't hardly re-watch the video of me shooting because my mom was shaking the camcorder so badly! I just remember going back to my hotel room, lying on the bed, and popping open a ginger ale without a care in the world. Having a soft drink was a celebration for me, because I wouldn't allow myself to drink carbonation, the months of the Hoop Shoot. I believed it may cause side cramps, so of course that was a no-no. I am not sure whether soft drinks really did or if I just used it as a persuasive measure to avoid sodas. Either way, it worked. Tonight, however, I would celebrate with a ginger ale!

At that evening's banquet, I was presented my trophy. The thing was huge, and I needed help carrying it down the stage steps. On the flight home, my trophy rode in my lap. People congratulated me and the airline recognized me when I boarded the plane. I was so proud.

So, why do I tell this long story? Well, the Hoop Shoot was one of the most defining experiences of my life. It taught me how to handle defeat, made me mentally tough, and required me to persevere. I felt that if I could win the National Hoop Shoot (out of a million kids) I could do just about anything. That was the moment I really started believing that with God, all things are possible! (Matthew 19:26) I knew nothing was too big for God ... even the dream of playing basketball at the University of North Carolina.

# Chapter 6

# My Siblings

*The heart of man plans his way,
but the Lord establishes his steps.*
— Proverbs 16:9

My sister and I have been super close forever as it's always been just me and her. We did school together, played together, took instrument lessons together, traveled together, and even played recreational league basketball together. There were a couple times, however, that we thought we were going to add some brothers or sisters. After I was born, my mom had a tubal ligation. Over time, the Lord convicted my parents of this decision, and they took to heart the passage "be fruitful and multiply." (Genesis 1:28) Mom and Dad felt they had given God control over every area of their life, except for the womb. They decided to make this wrong a right in 2007 and Mom had a tubal reversal. If it was part of the Lord's plan, Taylor and I were excited at the possibility of having another sibling. It wasn't but a few months later that Mom became pregnant. We were ecstatic, to say the least, and it was almost surreal that we were expecting a baby. All our lives, we had been asked the question, "Is it just you two girls?" After Mom received news of the pregnancy, so soon after the procedure, we were sure that it was the Lord's will for us to add to our family.

Since Mom was a bit older, we understood that there were some risks involved. So, the first few weeks, we were cautiously expectant. As the days wore on, we got more confident and more excited. Unfortunately, things took a turn for the worse and we lost the baby. My brother or sister was gone, just like that. Sadness and heartbreak followed. We had never met that little Church baby, yet we loved him/her so very much. All we could do now was wait for heaven and that grand reunion. It broke Mom's heart and I don't think anyone can understand the devastation unless you are the one carrying that soul. I know I couldn't hurt nearly as much as her. However, Mom is unwavering in her faith and knew there is a purpose in everything. She would have another miscarriage a couple of years later and we relived the heartbreak, once again. Why did the Lord lead my parents to have this procedure just to have two miscarriages? It just brought more pain and sorrow to our family. To this day, I still don't fully understand. I do know that out of those experiences, my mom started a ministry called *Remember Me,* which ministers to mothers who have lost babies. Sometimes God has us walk through a valley, so that something beautiful can bloom from it.

Afterward, my parents realized that we probably weren't going to have any more biological children and the Lord led them to pursue adoption. In 2010, we began the process of adopting internationally, specifically, two boys from Russia. There were mountains of paperwork, multiple home studies, and a hefty monetary cost for international adoption. I was hopeful and excited. I felt that with adoption, I was certain to get siblings. Surely, there were less risks involved than in pregnancy. After two times of believing I would be an older sister, I knew it was finally going to happen!

We waited for an over a year and finally got a referral! There were two brothers, ages 1 ½ and 3-years-old, who would be the perfect fit for us. With Russian adoption, we would have to travel to Russia twice before we could bring the boys home. Our family was scheduled to make the two-week trip over Thanksgiving, in 2012. Mom and Dad had picked out the names of the boys, with the oldest named Thad (my name if I had been a boy) and the youngest called Luke. The beginning letters of their names would match mine and Taylor's.

We spent the week before the trip packing for the cold tundra. It would be single digits, while in Russia. The flight was so long! We literally traveled across the globe and had multiple layovers and flights. Once we arrived, we stayed at a one bedroom, one bath, little apartment that was within walking distance of a small grocery store, pizza place, and (thank the Lord) a Cinnabon. We traveled two hours each day to visit the boys at the orphanage. They were precious and we were in love with them. Thad was blond-haired and had the sweetest spirit. He loved us playing with him and loving on him. Luke had brown hair and was a bit more timid than his older brother. However, he warmed up to us, as time went on. It was so hard to leave, but we knew once we had our court dates during our next trip to Russia, we could bring them home. We had their room ready upstairs with twin beds, decked out in a red and blue truck theme, as our homeschool room had been transformed into the cutest little room. As we were leaving these sweet boys and about to head back to the United States, Thad sang us a song about "sistra, mam i papa." It was precious and I couldn't wait to officially have these boys as my brothers. That was the last time I ever saw them.

The week after we got home, Vladimir Putin, the President of Russia, banned all Americans from Russian adoptions. Our adoption proceeding of Thad and Luke was terminated. My hopes of having siblings were shattered. We had a room upstairs with two empty beds that should have had held our boys. Once again, "Why?" I don't think I'll ever know, this side of heaven. God called us to pursue more children, yet each time He closed the doors. Maybe He wanted to see obedience or maybe He used us in someone's life along the way. Somehow, Mom knew before leaving Russia that we would never be back to get the boys. She wrote in her journal on the day before we left, "Whatever He will, in all of this, we will trust Him in it … whether or not He gives us the boys. If not, then we know He could have changed things and chose not. We will have walked in obedience. The outcome is up to the Lord." She would tell us later, "God told me in Russia that we would never get Thad and Luke and to finish strong with you, girls." Perhaps this wasn't so much about the boys, but rather about me and Taylor. Life was getting ready to intensify and the attention and needs were getting ready to turn back to the two of us. The Lord always knows. He is in tomorrow, and we must hold fast to His promises. God has a plan and purpose for our lives.

# Chapter 7

# On the Horizon

*Do not boast about tomorrow,
for you do not know what a day may bring.*
— Proverbs 27:1

Being homeschooled and a basketball player is a difficult combination when it comes to finding a team. Considering that there are no homeschool basketball teams in Wilkes County and homeschoolers weren't allowed to play on Christian school or public-school teams, finding a team was always a challenge. If I was going to play basketball, we were going to have to travel. The closest team was in Mt. Airy, about an hour and 10-minute drive from my house. I was 12 years old and this team, the Surry Runnin' Patriots, was a homeschool high school team. Practices were mid-morning on Tuesdays and Thursdays, so I would pack up my school things and do schoolwork while riding in the car. On the Patriots, I ended up starting every game and became the leading scorer, my first year. In 2010, the Mt. Airy Newspaper printed a featured article about me. When my coach was asked to comment on me, he said, "She has future goals of playing at UNC." That was for certain. I literally breathed basketball and did everything in my power to become the best I could be. Nothing was going to stop me.

That same year, at our national homeschool tournament at Liberty University, I was as sick as a dog. We were playing for 3rd place in our division, and I could not miss the game. Nonetheless, I woke up that morning so sick on my stomach that I couldn't eat or drink. I was shooting in the 3-point contest later that morning, as well. Fortunately, I was able to shoot in the contest and actually won the high-school division as a 12-year-old. I played in that tournament four years and never lost a 3-point competition. I thrived in the pressure-filled environment and contribute some of that success to the Hoop Shoot experience and being able to perform, while dealing with nerves. But, as the day wore on, I was getting weaker and could hardly walk. I couldn't keep anything down. We were playing at Liberty's huge arena, the Vines Center, and it took everything in me to make it down all the rows of seats to the court. I couldn't even do the warm-ups. The game was a blur, but I remember being right in the middle of a play and running off the court to the nearest trashcan. I threw-up and ran back onto the court before they blew the play dead. My coach saw what happened and subbed me out the next play. I was so weak and dehydrated that after the game my dad had to literally carry me out to the car. One thing that people could never doubt was my dedication to the game. I played two years with the Patriots and some changes were made, leading me to seek out another team with which to play.

The next couple of years, I played for the Carolina Cougars, a homeschool team based out of Winston-Salem. The Lord really provided that team when I desperately needed somewhere to play. The year I got there was the first year of the Cougars and the timing couldn't have been better. I was able to develop my game during those couple of years. However, the competition we played was not always as challenging as it needed to be. I was a sophomore in high school and by now, I was needing to get my name out there to college coaches. If you're going to play high-level, Division I basketball, you need to have your name on the radar no later than your sophomore year and I wasn't on anyone's radar. Other than attending UNC camp as a kid, I hadn't been very proactive in my recruiting. As I got older, I saw that the dream of playing at Carolina was going to be far-fetched and difficult. Not only would it be a challenge talent-wise or physically (I was barely 5'7"), but logistically and spiritually.

My parents had always believed that I was to be under their protection until I got married. Counter-cultural, I know, but they just couldn't envision dropping me off and saying good-bye to me for four years. So, I knew that my college situation and experience would have to be unique. I thought maybe we would combine playing basketball with distance learning to maintain the flexibility of being with my family. Too, I wasn't sure if basketball would even be an option for college since I had no plans to live, alone, on a traditional college campus for four years. I was so unsure of my future. In the meantime, my sister had been taking online college courses and graduated from Thomas Edison State College, by the age of 18, never having to leave home. At the time, this was the path I was on. I was taking college courses through CLEPs (College Level Exam Program), and I took my first college exam at the age of 12. I was racking up the credits and by the time I turned sixteen, I had 72 college credits. About that time, I told Mom I wanted to try and play Division I basketball in college. My parents supported me whole-heartedly, even though they were unsure as to how that would look. They trusted that if the Lord wanted me to play college basketball, He would provide in every sense, make a way for me to remain under their protection, and allow them to stay true to their convictions.

So, I started contacting colleges. I would email, send highlight tapes, my schedule, and other information to many of the Division I colleges, within three hours of my home. I even started a "BeRecruited" web page and loaded all my statistics. Of course, UNC was still my dream, so I would email each person on their staff, multiple times. It was around this time that Coach Hatchell had been diagnosed with leukemia. I was devastated for her. Although I didn't know Coach Hatchell personally, I had spoken to her each year at camp, and she was the face of UNC women's basketball. I sent her cards and messages letting her know I was praying for her. Thankfully, she beat the odds and defeated cancer.

Although deep down, I would have given anything to play at UNC, I knew I had to be more realistic and cast my net wide. If the opportunity to play at Carolina never arose, then I would have to decide if I wanted to play basketball anywhere else. I was having one of the best summer seasons of my life. We had played in the

USBA Nationals in Myrtle Beach, SC and won the championship. I hit 43 three-pointers over 6 games and averaged 28 points per game. I was hoping this performance would help me get on the radar of some colleges and I could gain traction in the recruiting process.

During this time, I had struggled with some severe stomach cramps during games and practice. At home, when I would condition on the treadmill, I would have to stop and curl up in a fetal position because the stomach pain was so intense. It would last about 10 minutes and then the pain would subside. My stomach was somewhat hard, felt like a rock, and was difficult for me to suck in. Honestly, I thought it may just be my abs and core. After all, I did work out a lot. But the pain associated with running got so debilitating that we scheduled an appointment with my doctor for Monday, August 4, 2014. I played in a local AAU tournament that same weekend and we had six games in two days. The cramps were severe and my stomach was bloated, but I was able to play and performed well despite the pain. Little did I know what was going on inside my body.

# Chapter 8
# The Shadow

*... in the shadow of your wings I will take refuge,
till the storms of destruction pass by.*
— Psalm 57:1

I laid back on the doctor's table and he felt my stomach. Immediately his face got grim, and he told me and my mom that he was ordering a CT scan and for us to go over to the Diagnostic Center for imaging. I had to drink that awful dye to "light up" my insides. The CT scan felt like my stomach was on fire! Afterwards, the technician said I needed to go straight back to my doctor's office. By then, I was getting concerned. There appeared to be too much urgency for it to be something minor.

I remember sitting in the waiting room after my CT scan and fearing what the doctor would say. Was it cancer? Was it a growth? What would lie ahead? Mom calmly told me, "Don't borrow trouble." It wasn't long before we were taken back again, and the doctor entered. He proceeded to tell us that I had a tumor and it looked to be substantial in size, like the size of a large grapefruit. I was shocked. How did this happen? How did I not know I had such a large tumor in my stomach? He proceeded to tell me that, as soon as possible, I would need surgery to remove the tumor. Surgery? I couldn't do surgery! I can't stand needles! How would I have an IV? How would I survive being cut open with a scalpel? As a little girl, I had run around the doctor's office, screaming to the top of my lungs, when threatened with the removal of a corn, from my foot. They had to hold me down and never could get me still enough to cut it off. This was the same girl who about passed out just watching my mom having blood drawn. Huh-uh! No, I just couldn't do surgery!

Well, I had no choice. I had a grapefruit size mass in my abdomen, and it was only going to get bigger the longer it stayed. Too, the doctors weren't 100% sure it was benign. I was scheduled to have an appointment at Brenner Children's Hospital in Winston Salem, the next day. During the appointment, the doctor scheduled my surgery for Thursday, August 7. I would be cut open from above my belly button to the top of my pubic bone and could expect to have about a ten-inch scar. Since it appeared the tumor was attached to one of my ovaries, it would need to be taken, as well. The plan was for me to have an epidural to manage the pain, and they would know in a week or so if the tumor was cancerous or benign. I would basically be bed-ridden for 6 weeks before I could start light activity. Basketball would be put on hold for months.

I had so many questions. How could I live with such a noticeable scar? I was only 16 years old. I would have to look in the mirror and see it every day, for the rest of my life. What about my ovary? I would be left with only one. Would it be more difficult to have children? What if something freaky happened to my only remaining ovary and I could never have biological kids? What if I never recovered enough to play basketball, competitively? What if the tumor was cancerous? What if, what if, what if? Isn't that what we so often do? We "what-if" our life away, when the Bible clearly says that we are to be anxious for nothing and 365 times instructs us not to fear.

This surgery was out of my control, and I was going to have to trust God with it. I had a supernatural peace and confidence the days leading up to it. I never even cried. I think my family was more worried than me. I remember Taylor sitting in her room crying the day before my surgery. She said she wished I didn't have to walk through this. I only got teary-eyed when I saw her crying because I didn't want her to be scared for me. Dad sent out emails to all his prayer partners and ministry supporters asking for prayer for my upcoming surgery. I had an outpouring of support from people all over and I knew heading into it that people were praying diligently for me. I knew God had a plan and I had peace in knowing that people would be praying. Although I didn't understand why this was happening, it was okay. I didn't have to understand. He gave me a peace that surpassed all understanding. "And the peace of God, which surpasses all understanding, will guard your hearts and your minds in Christ Jesus." (Philippians 4:7)

The morning of the surgery rolled around. I knew it wasn't going to be easy and I was already dreading the recovery. However, I also realized there were hundreds of people lifting me up in prayer and I could feel it. I went through the normal standard procedures beforehand, IVs and, because of the invasiveness of the surgery, the epidural. My parents and Taylor prayed with me right before I went back, and the next few hours were black. I woke up in the recovery room, in pain … lots of pain. Somehow, my epidural was not functioning correctly and had numbed the area above my incision, rather than the actual incision site. I was numb from my belly button to my neck, not my belly button down! I was in an excruciating amount of pain and in my dazed state I told the nurses I was hurting badly. I was in tears and praying out loud for relief. I was repeatedly saying, "Lord, help me. Lord, help me." I remember overhearing the nurses ask, "What is she saying?" and one replied, "I think she's praying." You better believe I was praying! Not too long after, they gave me medicine which reduced my pain. I asked for my Momma (Don't we all, when we are hurting?) and before I knew it, she was hugging me. I was told my tumor was 6.1 pounds and 11 inches long! Crazy! How did I survive carrying around a tumor the size of a baby, much less play six basketball games the weekend before? The incision ended up being a little over eight inches.

The days and nights that followed were a jumbled-up mess. I continued to struggle with the effects of my epidural malfunction and experienced some of the worst pain of my life. The nurses had given me a pillowcase that some ladies had hand-sewn and donated for kids at Brenner. The only one left was covered with little pastel bears and was for a baby. I didn't care. That pillowcase which covered my hospital pillow was a source of comfort for me. I named it "Friend." (To this day, "Friend" still sits on my bed, as a reminder that I can make it through anything.)

There were many times, during the hospital stay, that I would lay in the bed crying with Mom holding my hand. I felt so weak and began doubting if I would ever get back to normal and be able to play basketball again. There was one night that stands out in my mind. The second night after surgery, around 3 a.m., my pain became overwhelming and I was sobbing, shaking, and afraid. At that moment, I felt people praying and I believe God sent an angel to help and minster to me. "For he will command his angels concerning you to guard you in all your ways." (Psalm 91:11) I remember telling my mom, "I felt somebody praying for me." Not long after, the nurses were able to adjust the pain meds to exactly what I needed. I didn't experience another bout of pain like that again.

After that night, I continued to improve and was released from the hospital after a five-day stay. Within a week, we received the news that the tumor was benign! Praise Jesus! I was so happy to be home and I rested and healed. After six weeks, I began working to regain my strength. The next few months put my perseverance and mental toughness to the test. I returned to the basketball court a step slower and with what seemed to be an unbreakable wall with my endurance and stamina. Many times, I would be in tears after practice or a game. I struggled with discouragement and thinking I would never be in shape again or be as good. I feared failure. I was afraid of hitting that wall and showing weakness. I worked and worked, yet it seemed I wasn't gaining anything. I would run and get winded so easily. I would be in practice and my legs would feel like they couldn't move, and I could hardly put one foot in front of the other. I was discouraged as I always took great pride in being well-conditioned. Mom continued to tell me, "Give it a year." Meanwhile, I continued to fight this daily battle, while praying for strength. I knew God was still in control.

Months passed with what seemed to be little improvement. About 11 months later, at basketball practice, I felt like I broke through the wall, mentally and physically. I continued working hard to be in the best shape possible and get my explosiveness back. It took me well over a year and a half. Although I never thought it would take so long to recover and regain my strength, I realize that although it seemed like I was weak, the Lord was making me stronger, in many areas of my life. God used that experience to make me a stronger person, more reliant on Him, and to strengthen my belief in the power of prayer. Today, a lot of the everyday battles don't seem so severe. The Lord showed me and taught me a lot of things through a 6.1 lb., 11-inch tumor. So, whenever you are facing difficulties and perhaps wondering why God is making you walk through a storm, just know that He always has a bigger plan ... plans to prosper us and not to harm us ... plans to give us hope and a future. (Jeremiah 29:11)

That is my surgery story. It's an experience and a chapter that I thought would never be in my "Book of Life." At the end of the day, all I can say is that God is faithful. I'm thankful for my salvation in Jesus Christ so that when life's storms do come (and they always do) I don't have to walk through them alone. I love this quote from "The Hiding Place" by Corrie ten Boom, "No pit is so deep that He is not deeper still; with Jesus, even in our darkest moments, the best remains and the very best is yet to be."

# Chapter 9
# Recovery and Recognition

*I can do all things through him who strengthens me.*
— Philippians 4:13

Recovering from a major surgery is no joke. I played my first game after surgery three months later, on November 4, 2014. We didn't play the most competitive team on the schedule, but I had 44 points and hit 12 three-pointers, during that game. That part was nice, but I struggled. I felt so weak, and it was as if my legs weighed 100 lbs. each. I obviously didn't have my wind back and every time I got boxed out, it was a literal gut punch right in my incision area. The little bit of agility and speed I had before surgery was gone and I felt and looked like I was moving in slow motion. Nevertheless, I was grateful to be back on the court. Those couple of months after surgery were the longest I had ever gone without playing basketball. I had dealt with injuries and pain before (a severe ankle sprain, foot problems, stomach cramps, and sickness), but this was different. Day in and day out, I felt like there was no improvement and no increase in my stamina. I started working out with a local personal trainer in Wilkes to try and get back my conditioning. Oftentimes after an intense workout, I would feel like I was going to pass out and was zapped for the rest of the day. This wasn't like me as I used to be able to work out twice a day, shoot hundreds of shots at the gym, and still have enough energy for whatever was next.

Although it took me a year to fully recover, I learned the importance of perseverance and setting goals. I would run a mile on the treadmill almost every day and each day I would chart my time. The next day, I would have the goal of beating my previous time by one second. That doesn't seem like much, but it kept me pushing to be better, even if just by one measly second. Eventually, that one second turned into ten seconds and then twenty seconds until after months of setting these little goals, I was back running the time I had before my surgery.

One day, a year following surgery, I saw on social media where a guy had broken the world record for the most made three-pointers in 5 minutes, hitting 136. Now, I love challenges and I love doing hard things, so I thought to myself, "I have to try and beat this record." I asked my dad to rebound and my mom to video for me and off we went to my local YMCA to try and beat it. I knew it would be hard from the get-go. Shooting threes for five minutes straight is hard enough. But, shooting for five minutes, from the three-point line (at a 90% clip) is a whole other level of difficulty! Too, there could only be one rebounder and two balls. Poor Dad! He had to rebound all those hundreds of shots and then make accurate passes back to me. We had the two balls going at once, so if I missed a shot that was long off the back iron, we would have to restart from the beginning. I made it through several rounds of 5 minutes hitting 112, 115, 116, etc. I was getting so tired and losing strength in my legs and arms. I can't even imagine how Dad was feeling ... bless his heart. I stopped when I hit 120 threes in five minutes. That totaled one made three-pointer every 2.5 seconds at an 88% clip. It wasn't the record, and I was disappointed. Mom and Dad told me that it was still remarkable and that I should post it to social media, with the hope that it may help my recruiting efforts. I was hesitant, but I posted it.

It started out on my dad's Facebook page (my Facebook page wouldn't allow me to make it public, because I was too young). I got a lot of shares and people saying, "That was really impressive." Just for fun, I sent it out to ESPN. I didn't expect them to view my message, much less respond. I received a DM back reading, "Hey Leah, This is pretty great. espnW is interested in writing about this.

Would it be okay if one of our writer's contacted you? If so, what is the best way to get in touch?" I was elated! espnW is the ESPN branch just for women's sports. It was incredible that an affiliate to ESPN was sharing it! Sure enough, espnW posted my video and a story entitled *Watch High School Junior Leah Church Hit 120 3-pointers in Five Minutes.* Wow! I didn't think it could get much better until I scrolled through twitter and read a caption on ESPN's official twitter account with 21 million followers. It read, *Oh my buckets. A high school baller drained 120 3's in 5 minutes. WATCH:.* I remember flying out the back door screaming and running all the way up the hill to my grandparents' house to show them. I couldn't believe it. Isn't it every athlete's dream to get on ESPN?

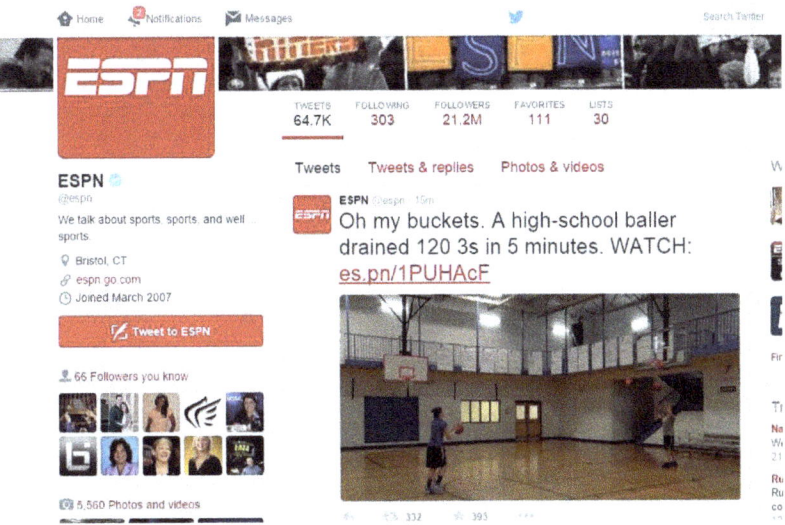

Soon after, SportsCenter shared it along with CBS Sports, USA Today, Fox Sports, NBA on TNT, Bleacher Report, and more. In addition, Fox 8 News, a local TV Station, drove up from Greensboro to video me shooting threes and to do an interview. I was on Cloud 9! Even though there were people on social media commenting, "Bet she makes a good sandwich," "Go get in the kitchen," "No one cares," "I could do that," "Women's sports are a joke," I was unfazed. I knew deep down that the people who commented stuff like that were the very people who probably couldn't hit 20 threes in 5 minutes, much less 120. Too, I tried to use that opportunity to point people to the Lord. Because my social media was getting a lot of views, I put John 3:16 in my bio. I couldn't have done it without the Lord's help, and it was only right He get the glory for it. I was so amazed that even though it wasn't the record, God still saw fit to use it for His honor. I learned a lesson that sometimes God just wants us to attempt things and give it our best. It doesn't have to be perfect, but often the Lord will bless our efforts. If you are afraid to attempt something hard or great, you may be surprised by what can be accomplished, if you just give it a try.

# Chapter 10

# The Preparation

*In all toil there is profit, but mere talk tends only to poverty.* — Proverbs 14:23

As mentioned, it was around this time that I decided to go through the recruiting process and see where that would lead me. According to the NCAA, only 1.3% of female high school basketball players go on to play Division I college basketball. Odds of success just aren't that high if you are average in a lot of areas. Starting out, I knew that it would have to be a God-thing for me to play Division I basketball, much less play at a Power 5, ACC school, such as North Carolina. I was a skinny, 5'8" (with basketball shoes on), homeschooler from little ol' Purlear, NC. I had sub-par speed and limited agility and jumping ability. I wasn't an all-star ball handler, passer, or defender. But one thing I had going for me is that I could shoot. I knew that if I was going to make it big, shooting would be the way I got there. So, I practiced shooting, shooting, shooting and some more shooting. Repetition after repetition. Thousands and thousands of shots. My dad would oftentimes rebound for me at the local high school gym and then I would come home and shoot some more. I bought a rebounding net which attached to my outdoor basketball goal so that I could get up more shots without having to chase after rebounds.

When I bought my Goliath basketball goal, it came with lights that attached to the top of the back board. I would run a drop cord from my garage and shoot well after dark. I was the happiest when I was shooting. I had so much motivation to be the best I could be, and I decided early on that no one would outwork me. In the back of my head, I always remembered the quote, "When you are not practicing, someone else is. When you meet them, they will win." And so, I worked.

    I created homemade workout equipment for myself. I constructed an agility ladder made out of strips of cardboard and string, push-up bars made from an old wooden rod and 2x4 blocks, a speed resistance parachute consisting of a contractor trash bag, string, and a backpack strap, and a defensive dummy-man made from a rake, 10 lb. Olympic weight, plastic lid, and a foam ball. My maw-maw and paw-paw gave me their old treadmill and I ran on it almost daily, until I burned out the belt, within a year.

    I was determined that at the end of my basketball journey, I would have no regrets. If I didn't make it to UNC or to Division I basketball, it wasn't going to be because of lack of work and effort. My parents emphasized Colossians 3:23 to me and Taylor growing up. It says, "Whatever you do, work heartily, as for the Lord and not for men." I was going to give basketball all I had and whatever happened after that was up to God.

    One experience that really helped me as a basketball player was working out with Ganon Baker. Ganon is a world-renown basketball trainer and has worked with numerous NBA, WNBA, and college players. We heard of him through a connection with my homeschool basketball team and scheduled a time for me to work out. I viewed multiple YouTube videos of him training and watched his clinics online to try and prepare for my workout session. We drove up to Bluefield, VA to an old YMCA about 2 hours and 15 minutes away. I was scheduled for a 2-hour workout. I thought that I was mentally tough, beforehand, but I walked out of that gym a whole lot tougher than I did going in. That workout was as intense as they come! Ganon had a different drive than anyone I had ever seen. He got after it, and you couldn't be around him if you didn't want that passion and swagger to rub off on you. Now, don't get me wrong, before I trained with Ganon, I worked hard, but afterwards I had a renewed vigor. I ordered a speed rope from Ganon's website and started jumping rope every day, began doing ball handling drills with tennis balls, did even more core and ab work, and worked on my flexibility. I was inspired to continue to outwork everyone else.

I was still playing for the homeschool team, the Carolina Cougars, when I was sending out all my information, basketball schedules, and statistics to every college coach within a reasonable distance from home. I would get email receipts from some coaches that said that my email had been read. This made me so excited, even though it really didn't mean anything regarding recruiting. However, time went on and I wasn't getting much interest from anyone. I guess you could say, I decided to go big or go home, so I called Coach Hatchell! They say nothing ventured, nothing gained. I was amazed when she answered and I was actually having a conversation with her. I was sweating and nervous and probably was a blabbering mess. Coach Hatchell said that she remembered me from camp, and I shared my schedule and team's information with her. She told me that she felt sure Coach Tracey (recruiting coordinator) would try to make it out to one of my games that season and hoped I could make it back to camp in the summer. I couldn't believe it! Carolina would really come and watch me play? I thought to myself that I would probably pass out if I saw Coach Tracey in the stands. How in the world could I possibly shoot and perform well? But that's what I wanted, right? I had dreamed of UNC watching me play basketball. Who knew if she would really be able to make it out to a game? Coach Hatchell could have said that just to be nice. After all, my season coincides right in the middle of their college basketball season.

Nevertheless, one night we were playing Burlington Christian and I was under the goal doing warm-ups when I saw a sight I will remember for as long as I live. In walked Coach Tracey, donned from head to toe in her Carolina blue sweat suit. I almost fainted. I looked up in the stands at my family and I think their eyes were bigger than mine. Before every single game I ever played, my mom would say a prayer with me. That night, I needed this prayer to be extra special. Coach Tracey was there to watch me and my unknown little homeschool team play. Honestly, the game was a blur. I don't even remember how I did. We won and I think I did average … not great, but not the worst. I do remember that I hit a buzzer-beater just inside half-court. That felt pretty good. I was in disbelief after the game. My parents, Taylor, and I went to eat at Mellow Mushroom afterwards and we were all just astounded. When something finally happens that you have wanted so much, it can be overwhelming.

I went home and ran up the hill to my grandparents' house and told them all about it. I was so happy. I guess one thing I should have guarded myself against was getting my hopes up. I don't know what I expected. I guess I had hoped that Coach Hatchell would call and offer me a full-ride scholarship the very next day. Ha! Days and months wore on and I realized that Coach Hatchell and Coach Tracey, (as the kind, Christian people they are) came to my game because they knew how much it meant to me. More than likely, they came as a gesture to someone who had faithfully attended their camps, emailed non-stop, and even sent cards in the mail. I started realizing that I just may not be good enough to play for UNC. Don't get me wrong, I wasn't giving up. But I started realizing that it would take the hand of God for me to get that chance. I even told my mom that if I could simply be on the team and shoot technical foul free throws, at least I would have fulfilled my dream to play for the Heels.

# Chapter 11
# Another Answered Prayer

*I will instruct you and teach you in the way you should go;
I will counsel you with my eye upon you.*
— Psalm 32:8

After my sophomore year, my team, the Carolina Cougars, disbanded. I was left without anywhere to play my final two years of high school. This was disheartening as those years were the most important of my recruiting process. As stated, it was challenging to find a place for a homeschooler to play competitive basketball. There were a few homeschool teams within about an hour and a half from home, but none that played a competitive enough schedule that would allow me to get in front of college coaches, as well as push me to become the best I could be. I sometimes tend to think catastrophically like, "I will never find a team to play on and thus, I will never be seen by college coaches and then I'll never get to play college basketball." I know better than to think this way because my mom always reminds me to, "Remember." I must remember all the times the Lord has made a way, remember all the times when it seemed He was late when He was right on time, and remember He's never let me down. Remember.

At the time, I was playing summer AAU. It was July and I had experienced a rather rough summer basketball season. My confidence was low as I had not been in the greatest environment. I had a coach that confronted me after I made a mistake on the court. During a timeout, she told me that no college coach would ever want me on their team. This was just one instance, but there were multiple others. I realize that some people respond positively to coaches degrading them, but I don't – at all! My love language is words of affirmation and I respond best to positivity and encouragement. I was so hurt and, unfortunately, I started internalizing those words. I really started believing that no one wanted me. I wasn't good enough. I wasn't big enough. After all, no college coaches had even shown any interest in me, at this point. Was all my hard work for naught? On top of that, I didn't even have a team in which to play, and the high school season started in a couple of months.

Once again, the Lord was preparing to show Himself strong. While continuing my AAU season at a tournament in Greensboro, NC, my dad had conversations with the former NBA and Wake Forest great, Delaney Rudd. My homeschool team had played his high school team, New Hope Christian Academy, who had been ranked top 10 in the nation. We got blown out, but I had a good game against them and scored 26 points, with 21 coming in the first half. So, Coach Rudd had recognized my dad and started talking about his team, stating they were changing locations, and were now Forest Trail Academy. He proceeded to tell my dad that if I ever wanted to come and play for him, he would have a place for me! Wow! Was this a coincidence? I think not! Dad explained to Coach Rudd that I would continue to be homeschooled through high school and therefore, would not be able to enroll in or attend another school. Coach Rudd said that shouldn't be a problem because his independent league did something similar to an online/homeschool program. So, it wouldn't be an issue for me to just continue with our homeschool and still play for his team.

I was elated to hear about this opportunity, but somewhat intimidated at the same time. This team was top-notch and probably one of the best high school basketball teams in the state of NC. They had multiple DI commits, including Coach Rudd's daughter, Lucky, who was committed to the NC State Wolfpack. We attended a practice at their gym in Kernersville, NC (1 hour and 20 minutes from my house) and spoke to Coach Rudd afterwards. Forest Trail's practice mimicked a college-level practice. The intensity was high, the talent and athleticism were out the roof, and I was impressed and terrified at the same time. I realized that I would know if I was college-level material after the first couple of practices with this team. Coach Rudd told us that they practiced every single day except Saturday and Sunday and played in tournaments all the way from NY to Florida. After hearing all of this, I didn't know if there would be any way for us to make such a great commitment. Talk about running the roads! This would require leaving my house every single day at 12:00 to arrive at the gym for a 2:00 practice, leave the gym around 5:00, drive home and get back around 7:00 or so. I had just gotten my license and my parents didn't want me driving that far by myself. Too, the expense of traveling to all those places was overwhelming. But my parents, again, told me they would make it happen.

We prayed about it and the Lord gave us peace about joining Forest Trail Academy's basketball team. It would prove to be one of the greatest decisions of my life. Coach Rudd was the best coach for which I could have ever have asked or hoped. He knew what I responded to and what I didn't and knew how to get the best out of me. I finally had a coach who believed in me, and I honestly would have run through a brick wall for him. Forest Trail prepared me so well for college basketball. I honestly think that most of our practices were harder than those in college. Although I wanted to quit after the first three days of practice, it made me mentally and physically tougher. My teammates were great, too. At my first-ever practice, Lucky, (Coach Rudd's daughter with the State commit) asked me where I wanted to play in college. I told her UNC. She didn't laugh or smirk like some of the reactions I had received in the past. It was as if she believed that I could possibly make it there and that meant so much to me. The Lord used Forest Trail and Coach Rudd as one of the biggest steppingstones in my basketball career. I'm forever grateful for that.

Coach Rudd also coached an AAU team, called the Lady Phoenix, and I played for them my last year of summer ball. An athlete's final summer is one of the most crucial times in the recruiting process. It especially was for me, as I had zero offers, going into it. I had generated some interest from some DII schools and a couple of mid-major Division I but hadn't received an offer. I guess you could say it was crunch-time and a bit of a "do or die" situation.

We played in some of the biggest showcase tournaments in the nation. It can be overwhelming when you walk into a convention center with over 75 courts, 500 teams, and hundreds of college coaches watching the games. That moment really puts into perspective how difficult it is to get offers to play college basketball, much less at the ACC-level. Each year, there's only so many spots that come open on a team. Considering my small pool of teams (as in mainly one, UNC), there were only 3-4 spots for my class. At a single tournament in Kentucky, there were thousands of girls my age wanting those couple of spots. Each game I played that spring and summer was pressure-filled, but I couldn't focus on how big the moment was or I would psych myself out. I had to constantly remind myself that I was ready for the moment and my path had prepared me for this. I had been through the Hoop Shoot experience, through a major surgery, and I had put in the time and reps. Nonetheless, it was an up and down experience. I would have a good game where I'd shoot the ball well, then a rough game where my shooting suffered. When there were coaches at our game (whether they were there to watch me or not), I wanted to perform well and sometimes wouldn't have my best showing.

One thing I tried to control was my attitude, my respect toward my coaches and teammates, and how hard I played. Ultimately, many of the coaches who recruited me said that they loved my shooting ability but liked my character even more. Don't be fooled to think character and respect don't matter because they do! Still, it was hard when I would have bad shooting games, as afterward, there were many tears shed in the car. I honestly felt like a complete failure and wanted to give up and quit so many times. I wanted perfection and could never attain that. I knew the Bible said to be anxious for nothing, but man, it was difficult when it felt like your whole future hinged on your performance, during those games. However, I learned that when God is in it, He can override any bad performance and any failure. There is nothing out of the Lord's hands or anything that catches Him by surprise.

There are two live viewing periods in April when college coaches can come and watch you play. I had a good showing during those periods and received my first two offers, from Elon University and then High Point University! I was so excited and honored! I had also gained some interest from NC State. Since my teammate, Lucky Rudd (the daughter of my coach), was committed to State, their coaches had attended several of our games, during our past season. They came to watch a few of my games during the April viewing period and then invited me to come to their camp that summer. The prospects of an ACC team showing interest in me was incredible, even if it was UNC's rival. I was honored to have college coaches interested in me and was grateful that God saw fit to give me opportunities at the next level. Deep down, though, I was holding out. Just hoping and waiting.

It was during that time that the Lord taught me to be grateful for the little things. I wrote this post on my Facebook page on June 4th, 2016:

> *I'm thankful for the lessons the Lord teaches us and for humbling us every now and then. Perspective is everything! I was at the Y the other day, shooting ball, doing my normal routine...you know, the things we do each day and don't really even take time to appreciate. Well, I was starting my under the basket shots, when I noticed a lady in a wheelchair shooting on the side goal...she would shoot the ball and it would come up several feet short and she would wheel herself over and retrieve the ball, reposition her wheelchair and shoot again and again. It really struck me deep and humbled me – here I was, blessed just to be able to walk, and have the strength to play a game I love, yet often times I don't even realize and appreciate it. That could easily be me in a wheelchair with a desire to play basketball, yet not physically being able to. I had to ask God to forgive me for all the times I lace up my shoes and pick up my ball without thanking Him for the ability He's given me. A lot of times, I get frustrated when I miss shots and*

*make mistakes yet I should just be thankful that I have the strength to shoot a ball, period – miss or make. I sometimes don't like the conditioning and running part that goes along with basketball, but I should just be thankful that God has given me legs that are capable of running. We take so many things for granted and don't even take the time to appreciate how much we are blessed. If we are able to stand and walk, we are more fortunate than a lot of others! God has given each of us a gift and equipped us to use our gift to the highest potential. Don't let it go to waste...you have health and ability for a reason. So, I'm asking the Lord to change my perspective...when I miss a shot, I thank Him that He gave my arms the strength to shoot it...when I run and get winded, I thank Him I have legs that can move and a heart that beats...when I make a mistake, I thank Him for giving me a mind that knows right/wrong, and when I get discouraged I remember His goodness and not my problems. If you think you have it bad, it doesn't take long to look around and see that someone has it worse. What you do daily and take for granted, others would give anything to be in your place...so sobering! I thank the Lord for this reminder and I hope that I'll live each day to the fullest and never take for granted how blessed I truly am! God give me a spirit of gratitude!*

*"And whatever you do in word or deed, do all in the name of the Lord Jesus, giving thanks to God the Father through Him."*
*-Colossions 3:17*

This reminder couldn't have come at a better time, as I had been dealing with sinus problems and headaches for several years. I went to a specialist in Winston-Salem and he diagnosed me with chronic sinusitis. I would have spells that would last for several months when I couldn't breathe out of my nose, and I would have sore throats and terrible headaches. Nothing seemed to help. My sister was into natural homeopathic remedies and honestly, I was willing to try just about anything. We started out by putting drops of essential oils in a pot of boiling water, draping a towel over my head, and breathing deeply. Then we graduated to a garlic soup-blend which consisted of chopped up garlic, bone broth, and cayenne pepper. If I didn't have sinus problems after that, I was bound to have stomach issues! Then came the ultimate remedy I will never forget. Taylor had me lie on the bed with my head hanging off, upside down and proceeded to squeeze a fresh cut lemon down my nostrils. I think I died for about two minutes and came back to life. I was convinced the burning sensation fried everything all the way to my brain. I looked at Taylor like she was crazy and asked where in the world she got the idea to squirt straight lemon juice up my nose. She said, "I read it somewhere." For anyone who doesn't think that could possibly hurt, go try it. Your nose will never be the same. Just kidding!

Taylor's research and suggestions were often very helpful. Over time and with some supplements and diet change, my sinusitis symptoms improved. I still struggle from time to time with some flare-ups, but I'm grateful that it's nothing more serious. Throughout my basketball career, my health always seemed to plague me — whether it was colds, headaches, stomach cramps, bugs, ankle sprains, etc. I even played with strep throat and couldn't swallow or barely breath, because my throat was so swollen. Then at a tournament in Washington, DC, I got food poisoning and was so sick that I laid on the bathroom floor all night beside the toilet. We were playing the next day and I couldn't miss it. Nonetheless, many people often have it a lot worse, and I have much to be grateful for. Thankfully the Lord sustained me through it all and allowed me to continue to pursue my dream of playing Division I basketball.

# Chapter 12

# The Sting of Reality

*For I know the plans I have for you, declares the Lord,
plans for welfare and not for evil,
to give you a future and a hope.*
— Jeremiah 29:11

Earlier that year, when I talked to Coach Hatchell on the phone, she mentioned about me coming back to UNC camp and was looking forward to seeing me. Of course, I made plans to attend that June, as this could be my chance to play in front of her and show that I belong at UNC. I enrolled in their elite camp (the first time in about two years, due to AAU tournaments). This year, however, I made it a priority to be in attendance. At each camp, you get a chance to take a photo with Coach Hatchell in your official camp t-shirt. I was able to speak to Coach Hatchell, briefly, and she told me she was happy to see me at camp. Mentally and physically, I was ready to show every coach at UNC that they needed me, and I could play at this level. I had prayed that I would perform well and felt sure that God would allow me to impress the coaches. After all, this was my dream and my big chance. Ah, but best-laid plans don't always come to fruition, do they?

It is the understatement of a lifetime when I tell you that camp was a disaster. I did awful. I struggled with intense cramping like the pain I had experienced with my tumor. Every time we would play 5-on-5 and scrimmage, I could only go for about 2 minutes before I had to sub out or just grind it out. I knew I was not playing to my full potential. I was ashamed, embarrassed, and devastated. The cramping was debilitating, and I couldn't understand what was causing it. Why did God let this happen? Didn't He know this was my big chance? You don't just keep getting opportunities to show coaches at your dream school what you can do on the court. Everything I had worked for all those years, the thousands of shots, the conditioning, the workouts with Ganon Baker, the traveling and expense, the physical pain to recover after surgery, was just thrown out the window in one weekend. Honestly, I didn't understand it and I was upset with the Lord. He could have allowed me to play well and catch the eye of every coach there. Instead, I failed.

I thought when I walked off Carmichael's court during elite camp, it would be the last time I would ever set foot on those beautiful Carolina blue hardwood floors. I distinctly remember looking up at the banner that hung above the doors of Carmichael. It read, "Playing at Carolina is an honor, Winning at Carolina is a tradition." I cried. I wouldn't get that honor. I had done everything in my power to achieve that dream. I had worked my bottom off, I had been assertive in the recruiting process, I had emailed and called coaches, and I had attended camp. I blew it. I wasn't good enough and it was time that I looked at other options and came to grips with it. Even my mom will tell you that after Elite camp, she thought it was over and had seen the last time she would watch me play on a Carolina basketball court.

I had to do some soul-searching after that weekend. Did I really want to play basketball in college, if it wasn't going to be at UNC? Would I ever be happy anywhere else? If the hopes of playing at Carolina were gone, where was I going to find my motivation to be the best, every single day? Too, what about my stomach cramps? I thought that my surgery corrected this. How could I ever play basketball in college with those debilitating cramps, every time I ran? I realized, however, that I loved the game of basketball way too much to give it up. I would see it to the end.

I figured that it would be easier if UNC was out of sight and out of mind. So, I packed up some of my Carolina t-shirts and some of the UNC memorabilia in my bedroom and put it downstairs in the basement. I had to start setting my mindset on reality. I still had a goal to play Power 5, Division I, basketball. Yes, deep down I wanted a miracle to happen and to be able to play at UNC, but ultimately, I had doubters to prove wrong. I had coaches who told me no one would want me, people telling me that I should be realistic in my college basketball choice, those who told me I was way too slow and didn't have the quickness to make a DI college team, and naysayers who told me that I was barely the height of a college point guard, much less a shooting guard. They told me that unless I could handle the ball better, I would never make it. There were those who said that because I was homeschooled, I would never make it. I felt that it was high-time I used the skeptics as my motivation. It is interesting that few people factored in the single, biggest advantage that I had on my side ... God! "But seek first the kingdom of God and his righteousness, and all these things will be added to you." (Matthew 6:33) Whatever God had planned for my life would happen and there was nothing and no one that was going to stand in His way. God has ordained each of our steps and nothing takes him by surprise. I love the lyrics to the song, *Way Maker*. "Even when I don't see it, You're working. Even when I don't feel it, You're working. You never stop, You never stop working. You never stop, Jesus. You are a way maker, miracle worker, promise keeper, light in the darkness. My God, that is who You are."

# Chapter 13
# Moving On

*Trust in the Lord with all your heart, and do not lean
on your own understanding. In all your ways acknowledge him,
and he will make straight your paths.*
— Proverbs 3:5-6

    I didn't have much time to lament my experience and performance at UNC Elite Camp. The following week I was signed up to attend NC State's Elite Camp. The State coaches had seen me play for Forest Trail when they came to watch Lucky and had invited me to camp. I wasn't in the greatest of mental states to attend because I was so worried that my stomach would cramp, again. The last thing I wanted was to end up with a performance that would mark me off another team's list. We prayed and prayed for my stomach not to cramp and for me to be able to play to the best of my ability. I've got to admit that walking into NC State's gym and being surrounded by all the red was a little odd for this die-hard UNC fan. But I ended up having a good camp and my stomach was very manageable. Instead of hurting my cause by attending camp, I felt like I probably improved it. After camp, we went to eat at a local deli, on NC State's campus, and my parents asked me if I could see myself going there. Maybe this was the Lord's plan after all. I obviously had had the worst performance possible at UNC and everything just felt off, but here at State, I had a successful camp and felt pretty good about the place. Obviously, though, I was miles and miles away from even having a chance to play for the Wolfpack and didn't even know if they would want me.

    However, an invite to camp is just a formality and something coaches offer if they are remotely interested in a player. For example, the year before, I had gotten an invitation from Duke's assistant coach to come to their elite camp. He had heard about me through a coach my team played against in AAU and wanted to see me play. So, although it went against everything in this lifelong Tar Heel fan, I attended their camp. Surprisingly, I had one of the best camps of my life and did very well. To kick things off, I won a shooting challenge (as their head coach looked on) and then won a core/plank challenge to see who could hold a plank (a core strength exercise) the longest. Out of over 100 girls, I held the plank the longest at 4 minutes and 30 seconds. Too, I won their free throw competition and got an offensive award at the end of camp. I honestly couldn't have played better. However, I guess I didn't pass the eye test or just wasn't what they were looking for, because I never heard anything from anyone at Duke, again. Ironically, the Duke camp gave out scrimmage jerseys, with random numbers and mine at Duke was #20. That number would hold some significance down the road.

Back to the question of whether I could see myself at State. If UNC was not an option, then, yes, I could see myself playing for NC State. After all, they were in the ACC conference, a Power 5, Division I school and a great program. Wasn't that what I wanted? Now, it was just a waiting game to see if I got an offer to play there. I still had the July recruiting period and some big tournaments to play. NC State said they would be watching me and stayed in touch. I was honored to even have an ACC school interested in me. Too, it didn't hurt that my head coach's daughter was going to play there.

As mentioned, the month of July's live recruiting period was a bit up and down for me. I was excited that I had picked up a couple more offers from UNC-Charlotte and UNC-Greensboro! However, I hadn't had much interest beyond that. I was running out of time and opportunities. I had done the best I could with what the Lord had given me. I was only so tall and so athletic. If it wasn't enough, it just wasn't enough. The reality of that would be difficult to accept and I knew that I would have to guard against feeling like a failure, for the rest of my life. But it is what it is. Now that the viewing period was over, I would just wait and pray. It was after that July that I gave it to the Lord and told Him to do with my basketball career whatever He wanted. It was obvious that my best laid plans of playing for UNC were out of the picture, so whatever His will revealed, I was good with it. Isaiah 55:8-9 says, "For my thoughts are not your thoughts, neither are your ways my ways, declares the Lord. For as the heavens are higher than the earth, so are my ways...." It is interesting that oftentimes in life, it takes coming to the point of surrender and contentment before you see the Lord working. He's always working on our behalf; we just don't necessarily see it until later.

I am not always great at waiting and being patient and it's something I continue to work on. So, when I saw a chance to attempt to break a record, I jumped at the opportunity. I had seen on Facebook where an Arkansas men's basketball player held the record for the most made 3's in one minute ... 27. I really felt like I could beat that score. As it ended up, I was able to beat it by hitting 32 threes in a minute. Of course, it wasn't an official Guinness Record (as I didn't have a representative there to watch), but even to this day, it hasn't been beat. The next highest is 31 makes. I posted the video and once again espnW shared it, then Sports Illustrated, Fox Sports, House of Highlights, USA Today, and more. Not everyone has a video go viral once in their life, much less twice. It was so neat, and I rode the high for a time. It's funny how things like this are amazing for a while. You are living the dream with the notoriety and pats on the back, but before long, everything settles down and fades away. It's like that with anything in life, which is why there is no lasting fulfillment except that which is found in Jesus and doing things that will last for eternity. Don't get me wrong, accomplishments are great and can be used for His glory and to point people to Him. But, if our identity is found, solely, in what others think about us and say about us, then we will be empty and unsatisfied.

# Chapter 14

# Seeing Red

*Remember not the former things, nor consider the things of old. Behold, I am doing a new thing; now it springs forth, do you not perceive it?*
— Isaiah 43:18-19a

During this time, I had been talking back and forth with NC State. The coaches showed quite a bit of interest in me and considering the type of offense than ran, they felt I could really help them as a pure shooter. The prospect of getting a chance to play in the ACC was so exciting and I was hoping and praying for an offer. One day, Coach Rudd told me and my family that Coach Moore would be giving me a call soon. I could only hope this would be the call telling me he wanted me. I waited and waited for that call. A day went by and then another. I kept my phone with me 24/7 with the ringer up, as loud as possible. I wasn't about to miss, potentially, the most important call of my life.

Almost a week went by and finally, my phone rang. Coach Moore popped up on the ID. I will always remember when and where I was when that call rang through. It was a Wednesday night, and I was sitting in church listening to my Uncle Bubber preach (his name is Kevin, but as a little girl, my mom called him "Bubber", and the name has stuck). I ran out the side door as fast as I could and answered my cellphone. I've got a habit of pacing when I am on an important call, so I walked behind our church past our church's playground all the way up to the cemetery. Coach Moore explained to me that they did, in fact, have a spot for me on their team for next season and wanted me to join the Wolfpack. They liked how I played and my shooting ability. He said that it would have to be a preferred walk-on position, which meant that for at least the first year, I would pay my way with no financial assistance. If a scholarship became available, I could be offered one, but nothing was guaranteed. Deep down, I had hoped for a miracle of being offered a full scholarship, but I was more than grateful that NC State would even give me the opportunity to play for them. To this day, I'm still thankful for their willingness to offer me a spot on the team and for the chance to play at the ACC level.

I told Coach Moore I would talk to my family and get back with him. I knew deep down what decision I would make. I wouldn't be able to pass up the chance to play in the ACC. Even so, I was disappointed at the financial prospect, because I hated for my parents to have to bear the brunt of the costs. As I mentioned before, I am very money-conscious and tight (even if it is my parents' money). I could still choose one of the other schools that had offered me a full scholarship, get a free education, and play basketball. I told my parents this, but they knew my dream of playing at the highest level and once again told me, with the Lord's help, they would make it happen. They had already sacrificed so much for me to even be in this position but were willing to see it through.

A day or so later, we called Coach Moore and I put him on speaker phone. I told him I wanted to come play for NC State. He was glad to hear it and asked me to come visit one day the following week. I had never even been to NC State, except the one time I was at elite camp. Even then, I had not seen their game gym. We had a beach trip planned with my extended family the week Coach Moore asked us to visit, but we told him we would make the trip back to Raleigh. Once on campus, I got to tour all their facilities, including the newly renovated Reynolds Coliseum. It was extremely nice. There were lots and lots of red, especially for someone who was raised with an aversion to that particular color and team. I got to speak with all the staff members, and they were nice and seemed glad that I would be attending State. We had a meeting with Coach Moore, and he explained how things worked as a preferred walk-on and other information pertaining to the team. At one point, Coach Moore asked for my email, and I awkwardly told him it was: leah.tarheel@gmail.com. Cringeworthy, I know. I played it off explaining that this had been my email address since I was 8 years old, and I just hadn't gotten around to changing it. Wow! I really started out on a good footing, right?

I would be part of the Pack now and I was excited. But, boy, it was different and something I would have to get used to. At the beginning of September 2016, I announced on social media that I would be attending and playing basketball at State. People were shocked that a lifelong, die-hard, UNC fan was going to play for the Pack. Honestly, I was shocked too. All my NC State friends were pumped while the Tar Heel fans asked, "Why not Carolina?" It was hard to respond, but I explained that I hadn't received an offer from them and wasn't being recruited. I remember my mom and I discussing the turn of events and wondering why things were  turning out as they were. Why did I attend Carolina camp all those years? Why did I develop relationships with some of the UNC people? Why did I always dream of playing for UNC, only to end up going to NC State? What purpose did the Lord have in it all? We chalked it up to perhaps the relationships made during the early years would hold significance down the road with the hope that we made a positive impact on someone along the way. We're not God, so I don't reckon we were supposed to understand.

I went to Dunham's Sports and purchased my first ever NC Shirt and hoodie. We painted over my Carolina blue walls in my bedroom and chose a neutral white color. I took down the pictures of me, when I was seven, with Tar Heel great, Ivory Latta, and the picture of me and Taylor with Roy Williams. We packed up all my remaining UNC stuff and took it to the basement. I won't lie, that was a little bit tough, and I had a pang of sadness. But it was time to start shifting my mind and my loyalties. I had a renewed vigor and work ethic. I put on my NC State hoodie and headed to the YMCA to get my shots up. "Go Pack," I told myself....

I had to notify the coaches at the schools that had offered and recruited me to let them know that I would be playing for State. Those calls are never easy because I had developed some good relationships with many of those coaches. Plus, I so appreciated them offering me and wanting me on their team.

I began setting up my NC State portal information and researching what I might want to major in at State. I was very relieved that I finally knew where I would be attending the following year and that the recruiting process was over. It had been a long and somewhat stressful year and a half, and I was happy I would be able to play my senior year knowing I would be playing in the ACC, next season. Forest Trail had their "boot camp" in August, and we would practice twice a day and lift. Practice consisted more of conditioning and strength training than basketball skills. It was tough and mentally and physically exhausting, but I had so much confidence and energy stored. I was eager to work, because I would be playing Division I, Power 5 basketball, very soon, and I wanted to be ready!

# Chapter 15

# A Dream Come True

*God is not man, that he should lie, or a son of man, that he should change his mind. Has he said, and will he not do it? Or has he spoken, and will he not fulfill it?*
— Numbers 23:19

A month passed. Then one day, everything (the entire trajectory of my life) changed. An email came through on Mom's computer. It was an email that I had been waiting on and hoping would come ... for years. The sender? Coach Tracey Williams-Johnson, recruiting coordinator and assistant coach at the University of North Carolina. Simply put, Coach Tracey said they had seen where I made a verbal commitment to NC State and asked if my mom could call her. I couldn't believe my eyes. What? I hadn't heard from them in months ... and I had plans to go to State. I mean, UNC was totally out of the picture. Did they just want to congratulate me on my commitment or ask why I chose NC State or what? Could there be a possibility that they could offer me a walk-on spot at Carolina? No, that couldn't possibly happen. That would mean my dream would come true and that only happens at Disney World!

My mom called Coach Tracey and she said that Coach Hatchell was "devastated" that I took a walk-on with NC State and had no idea I would have even accepted a walk-on spot. She told Mom that Coach Hatchell wanted her to call. The next day, Mom talked with Coach Hatchell about one thing and the next (her newly released book, faith, etc.) and then she asked about me. Mom explained to her my love for UNC, but that when State offered me, Carolina was out of the picture. Mom then handed me the phone to talk to Coach Hatchell. She told me right there, at that moment, that she could match State's offer with a walk-on spot and would have to talk to her staff on Monday (this was a Friday) to see if a scholarship might be in the picture. Coach Hatchell wanted us to come for a visit that Monday and we told her we would. However, after we talked to my high school coach, he suggested that we wait until after their meeting on Monday to hear their offer. He was a bit worried since UNC wasn't a done deal and it may jeopardize my offer with NC State, leaving me with nothing. We decided to wait and hear what they said on Monday before we visited.

At the end of the day on Monday, we hadn't heard anything from UNC, and I was stressing out, BIG time. I texted Coach Tracey and she said that they had been busy and hadn't had time to call. Coach Tracey felt sure my spot would be a walk-on, but that Coach Hatchell really wanted to see me face-to-face. I sure wasn't about to mess this chance up with UNC, so I said we would come for a visit that Thursday. I was disappointed that they had decided it would probably just be a walk-on spot, but I was super excited because it was Carolina … my dream school!

My dad was on a mission trip to Haiti, so on Thursday, my mom, Taylor, and I went to Chapel Hill. I honestly didn't know what to expect. I could only hope for a chance to walk-on. I had been keeping up with their roster situation and knew that they had already filled three spots with freshman commitments for that year and didn't have but one opening available … if that. The visit was like a blur and the details all run together for me. That morning, Coach Tracey took us on a visit around campus in their golf cart. We had seen on the daily schedule that the very last thing was a meeting with Coach Hatchell in her office. I found myself on the visit just wishing that it was time to talk with her. I had to know what was on the table. I vaguely remember Coach Tracey taking us to the Old Well and sipping out of the fountain of that well-known landmark. Coach Tracey snapped a picture of me, my mom, and sister. To this day, it is still my mom's screensaver picture on her cellphone.

Of course, I had probably been on campus more than fifty times, but this time was different. I was riding in this snazzy, blue Carolina golf cart with a UNC women's basketball coach. On our drive, we even stopped to talk to a Christian leader on campus. It was really neat to see that this was a priority to Coach Tracey. The faith of the UNC coaches was admirable and another reason I dreamed of playing for them. It would be amazing to have Christian coaches who would support and back me up in my faith in Christ! We also stopped and talked to the team's academic advisor and the team's chaplain. I was trying to soak in every minute, but at this point I was just about to go crazy. Was it almost time to talk to Coach Hatchell? Finally, the moment arrived.

After our tour, we walked into the women's basketball offices and waited a few minutes before we went into Coach Hatchell's office. Then, the door opened and there was Coach Hatchell. We walked into her office which was filled with Jordan shoes, trophies, awards, books, and pictures galore. Mom, Taylor, and I sat down on her couch and Coach Hatchell sat in a chair across from us. I couldn't believe that moment was real. I was sitting in Coach Hatchell's office, face-to-face with the legend herself. We small-talked a little and then Coach Hatchell began telling us that she had had me on her mind for weeks now. She said that she had seen in her desk drawer the cards I had sent her while she was battling leukemia. Coach Hatchell shared that for the past two weeks she couldn't get me off her mind. She had gone to bed thinking about me and would wake up thinking about me. She said that she even told her husband, Sammy, that she just couldn't get Leah Church out of her head. Then, she uttered the words that changed my life. "Leah, the Lord told me that I needed to offer you a scholarship to play basketball at the University of North Carolina and all you have to do is say, 'Yes.'" Tears. Tears. And more tears. Lord, could this moment be real? Everything I had dreamed of and worked for all these years ... all the sacrifices I and my family had made ... the hours spent running up hills and shooting thousands of shots ... the moments of wanting to quit and being told I wasn't good enough or tall enough or athletic enough … the coach who told me that no one would ever want me … the little girl who wrote in her family newspaper that one day she would play for UNC. The dream I held onto since I was 7 years old all came to fruition in that one moment. I looked at Coach Hatchell with tears in my eyes and choked out the words, "Yes!!! This is a dream come true and I can't thank you enough." Coach Hatchell said that we must have been doing a whole lot of praying because God told her to, "Get this kid to Chapel Hill!" She told me that I was special, and perhaps now, she could get some sleep! There was so much gratitude in my heart, and I was overwhelmed. I was overwhelmed by the Lord's goodness and faithfulness.

Coach Hatchell called in Coach Tracey to start drawing up the NLI (National Letter of Intent) papers for me.  She looked at Coach Hatchell a little surprised. I'm not sure if Coach Hatchell had shared with anyone what she was about to do. She told Coach Tracey, "Yes, I offered Leah a full scholarship." We went into Coach Tracey's office and started filling out papers with academic information. She was so happy for me. This was the end of October and the NLI signing period was up in about one week, so we would be pushed to get everything lined up and ready before then. I couldn't believe that I would get to sign a National Letter of Intent. Preferred walk-ons don't get to sign one, because there is no financial aid agreement. However, now that I was getting a full ride to the University of North Carolina, I would get to sign the NLI.

The team had practice about 30 minutes later and we watched while Coach Tracey continued to work on the information and papers. After practice, Coach Hatchell told the team and the rest of the coaches that I would be playing for Carolina next season. I was included in their after-practice circle, and even today, it seems surreal. After practice, I took a picture with all the coaching staff. I had worn a teal Nike shirt during my visit, but in hopes that I would leave Chapel Hill as a Tar Heel, I had packed a UNC jacket. I threw on my jacket and stood with MY coaches as Taylor snapped the pic. I remember getting to my car and calling my dad. He cried, I cried, we all cried. All we could say is "The Lord is good!" Dad told me he was so proud of me.

Yes, I had put in all the work, and I had given it my all. I gave my dream my best shot. But ultimately, it was the Lord. Simple as that. I heard it straight from Coach Hatchell's mouth, "The Lord told me to offer you a scholarship to play at UNC." Nothing can stand in the way of God's purposes. "Many are the plans in the mind of a man, but it is the purpose of the Lord that will stand." (Proverbs 19:21) It didn't matter that I wasn't 6 feet tall or had subpar agility for ACC level basketball. It didn't matter that I came from a hometown in which no other girl had ever played Power 5, Division I basketball. It didn't matter that I was homeschooled. It didn't matter that I wasn't a McDonald's All-American and never went on an official college visit. It didn't matter that the odds were stacked against me. It didn't matter what anyone said or believed about me. It didn't matter that there were only four spots open on Carolina's team and thousands of girls vying for them. It didn't matter that I was a nobody. God can take anyone and do the impossible. The Lord loves doing the impossible because it shows how mighty He is. Don't be discouraged by a big dream because we serve a big God. I was finally a Tar Heel! This was the best day of my life!

# Chapter 16
# Celebration

*Praise the Lord! Praise God in his sanctuary;
praise him in his mighty heavens! Praise him for his mighty deeds;
praise him according to his excellent greatness!*
— Psalm 150:1-2

The next day I called Coach Moore and told him I had been offered a full scholarship by UNC and would be attending Carolina. That was a tough call, as I was so appreciative for the opportunity he had given me. But, because of the way the Lord had moved and orchestrated things in Coach Hatchell's life, I knew in my heart that this was His plan for me. Yes, in my mind it seemed like God was late, but He doesn't move and work on our timetable. It reminds me of Lazarus in the Bible. The Bible says that after hearing about Lazarus' illness, Jesus waited two more days before leaving for Bethany, where Lazarus (and his sisters, Mary and Martha) lived. By the time Jesus made the journey and arrived in Bethany, Lazarus had been dead for four days. I'm sure Mary and Martha wondered how Jesus could just let their brother die. But He had a bigger plan and one that would show His glory even more-so than healing Lazarus. Instead of healing him from his sickness, Jesus raised Lazarus from the dead! Sometimes the Lord allows things to happen and go so far that only a miracle can change it. Oftentimes, in my life, I have found that the Lord waits until the last minute. Why? I think it builds our faith and it shows us that our timetables are not the Lord's. He sees the big picture and holds our lives in His hands. When I get discouraged or frustrated with where I am in life, I look back and remember all the times the Lord has come through for me.

I announced on social media that there had been a change of plans and that I would be a Tar Heel next season. I posted a picture of me and Coach Hatchell at my first year of UNC basketball camp when I was seven years old and titled it, "Dreams do come true." There was an outpouring of support from family and friends. Anyone who knew me, knew just how big of a Tar Heel fan I had always been, and many were happy to see my goal and dream come to fruition. My paw-paw and Uncle Bubber were especially happy. They both played college basketball at Gardner Webb but were die-hard UNC fans. Uncle Bubber attended UNC camp when he was young and one of his fondest memories was winning the free-throw competition and getting to shake Dean Smith's hand afterward. I have so many memories of watching UNC games with them while growing up and shooting ball in the back yard on Paw-Paw's old basketball goal (complete with a Tar Heel blue backboard). While they were supportive and happy for me when I told them that I was going to State, I know deep down it was a bit disappointing. They knew my dream and how much I loved Carolina. Uncle Bubber later told me that it was a weird and very awkward feeling when he and Paw-Paw went to buy NC State ball caps for the first time. Being a life-long UNC fan, it's just hard to immediately flip that switch and put all those feelings aside. That's why I was so excited when I got to tell them how the Lord had worked it all out and I was getting a full ride to play basketball at THE University of North Carolina!

My parents planned a signing day ceremony for me at Mt. Pleasant Baptist Church, our home church. They have a large gymnasium, and we invited a lot of our close friends and family, as well as my Forest Trail team and coaches. We decked the place out in Carolina blue and everyone who came sported something UNC. It was a glorious night. I shared the story of how things came to be and showed some pictures from my basketball journey. Mom and Dad also spoke, and it was a tear-jerker of a night. It is just a different feeling when you pour your heart and soul into something for so long and you finally reach the top of that high mountain. I signed my NLI as everyone looked on and experienced an overwhelming sense of gratefulness and awe of God's goodness. Many people have goals, ambitions, and dreams, yet never get the opportunity to achieve and fulfill them. God saw fit to let me live my dream and honored the work I had put forth throughout all those years. I wasn't going to stop there though. I would work and do my absolute best while at UNC and use the platform God gave me to impact and inspire as many people and kids as possible. I was ready to get started!

# Chapter 17

# The Journey Begins

*But they who wait for the Lord shall renew their strength;
they shall mount up with wings like eagles; they shall run
and not be weary; they shall walk and not faint.*
— Isaiah 40:31

My final season at Forest Trail was a success. We won many tournaments, including a championship win in Washington, DC, beating a top-five team in the nation. Unfortunately, I ended up badly hurting my ankle near the end of our season. I came back to play in one final tournament in New York but suffered a re-injury. A subsequent MRI revealed two torn ligaments in my ankle. I would have to rest it for 4-6 weeks, which meant my season was over. I missed out on my senior night and final tournament in Myrtle Beach but turned my focus towards rehabbing and getting my ankle strong for UNC.

I also was still dealing with intense stomach cramps throughout the season, similar to those at Carolina camp and before my surgery. We went to different doctors to try and find out the reason I cramped when running and exercising intensely. It made no sense. The cramping should have been gone since the tumor had been removed from my abdomen. Because of the invasiveness of that size of a tumor, my surgery doctor suggested that it could have displaced some of my organs and that scar tissue adhesions could be the issue. Unfortunately, without surgery, there were no tests and no way to determine the presence of scar tissue. No other doctors had any other solutions, so we decided to move ahead with the scar tissue removal at the end of March 2017. I would be enrolling in summer school at UNC in June and starting summer workouts.

Although I was nervous to have a surgery this close to leaving for school, I was just as nervous to have to deal with cramping at Carolina. It was a catch-22. What if I struggled to bounce back from this surgery like I did the last one? The doctor assured me that this surgery wouldn't be anything like the previous and I would be back to normal and hopefully cramp-free, within four weeks.

The surgery revealed a substantial amount of scar tissue in my lower abdomen. The doctor said that I should know whether this was the cause of cramping when I was recovered enough to run. As soon as I felt up to it, I went downstairs to my treadmill and ran a mile. Towards the end of the run, I felt the cramping coming on. My heart dropped. The surgery didn't fix it. What would I do? How do you play Division I basketball when your stomach cramps almost every time you condition and step on the court? Everything you do in college basketball is intense, plus I knew when I got to UNC, we would be training for our mile-run conditioning test. I couldn't even finish running a mile on my treadmill at home, much less on a track at UNC, with so much on the line. So, we prayed. We prayed for the Lord to take away the cramping. But He didn't. So, we prayed for the Lord to sustain me and get me through each day and each cramp.

I really battled anxiety. I knew before every conditioning session, every mile-run, and every practice, I would cramp. My stomach cramps were always worse in the morning and guess what? In the summer, we practiced and conditioned at 6:00 each morning. I remember the first practice I ever had was scheduled for 6 a.m. in the Smith Center's practice gym. We couldn't practice in Carmichael due to summer camp season and the use of our gym. My freshman year, I lived in Ram Village which is located above the Smith Center about 0.25 miles away. I set my clock for 4 a.m. because I needed that time to try and prevent my stomach from cramping. I would heat up a water bottle and place it on my stomach and do some stretches. Then, I would eat something containing some carbs and protein and hydrate. I would read my Bible, pray, and then walk down to the Smith Center to get taped. I got there at 4:45 a.m., even before my trainer. I was extremely nervous. This was my first practice as a Tar Heel. What if my teammates showed me up and I couldn't compete and play at this level? What if I didn't make any shots? What if my stomach started cramping? So many what ifs ran through my head.

I was the first one to get taped and out onto the court. There wasn't even anyone there with basketballs, yet, for me to get shots up. Most people lose the habit of showing up early over time and the newness wears off. Not me. My athletic trainer, Nicole, learned to expect me first thing as soon as her doors opened. I had to get my ankles taped and ready so I could get shots up early before practice. I was wired this way. I just had to get in extra work and show my coaches I deserved to be there.

The first practice was intense, but good. Once I started playing, all the "what if's" weren't at the forefront of my mind, and it was time to just play basketball. Thank the Lord my cramping wasn't bad and disabling. Unfortunately, every practice wasn't this way, and I would have to struggle through. I hated the cramps not just because of the pain, but because it made me look weak and worthless. I hated for my coaches and teammates to see me this way because I couldn't bear the thoughts of them perceiving me to be a slack or using it as an excuse to cop-out. That wasn't me at all and I took pride in my work ethic and determination. My stomach cramps were something that I begged God to take away from me, but until then, I would just have to do my best and rely on Him to sustain me. I knew one thing: He was making me stronger for it.

After practice was over, I took time to let it sink in that I had just practiced for the University of North Carolina and Coach Sylvia Hatchell! Jaelynn (my fellow freshman teammate) and I took pictures of each other standing outside the Smith Center in our UNC practice jerseys for the very first time. We had to hustle and get back to our dorms, because we had summer school classes at 9:30 and then worked Coach Hatchell's basketball camp the rest of the day.

I loved working basketball camp. Several of my teammates didn't like it, but I thought it was the best thing ever. You see, I was one of those campers that for years dreamed of being one of the UNC players. Every year I would go back to Granville Towers after camp ended and stand in line to get the players' autographs. They were my heroes! To have the opportunity to impact these kids and be someone they admired was such an honor for me. Now kids were standing in line to get *my* autograph! Just a few years earlier, I was in their shoes. I took every chance I could to talk to the kids and encourage them. I felt like God had given me this platform to help and inspire others. I couldn't let it go to waste!

Camp season was always one of my favorites. But those days were long. We would have 6 a.m. practices or weights/conditioning, class, followed by camp until about 9:30 p.m., and then we would often have pick-up games in Carmichael until 11:00 or midnight. I didn't have a car and didn't want to inconvenience my older teammates to drop me off, so I would run back, by myself, to my dorm after pick-up. It was just a little under a mile away, but as a freshman, I hadn't learned all the short-cuts. The first time I ran it, I'm pretty sure I went a good quarter of a mile out of my way, but over time I figured out the shortest, most efficient path. Those were some tiring days, but I loved it. I was living my dream and still in awe that I was there, at UNC.

# Chapter 18
# Not All Fun and Games

*Commit your work to the Lord,
and your plans will be established.*
— Proverbs 16:3

There's making it to Carolina on a basketball level and then there's making it to Carolina on an academic level. This is where I must sing my mom's praises. All students who want to play college sports must be approved by the NCAA Clearing House. It is somewhat of a bear and homeschoolers must jump through even more hoops than the average student. Along with transcripts and stacks of documents, there were tons of information required. To top it off, NCAA stipulations were separate from the UNC admissions requirements. Mom worked diligently, for weeks, pulling together the necessary information and ultimately, I got approved to play in the NCAA and accepted to the University of North Carolina. I was officially the first homeschooled women's basketball player to play for UNC. That was so cool!

The first time I ever set foot in a classroom setting was my first class in summer school. I would jump in headfirst at UNC! I was a little bit worried about the academics, at Carolina. I knew the university was very distinguished and their classes were known to be difficult and rigorous. I didn't consider myself the smartest in the world, but Mom always told me that if I knew how to learn, I would be fine wherever I went.

Throughout my homeschool journey, we always prioritized experiences over sitting in front of a book. Now don't get me wrong, we did a lot of book learning and covered all our subjects. But Mom always said, "Life is school," and bookwork was to come alongside living. So, if there was a day that we needed to pick green beans out of our garden and can them, then that was school for the day. Or if Dad and I went deer hunting one morning, then learning was taking place. Too, Mom emphasized the importance of reading. She said if we could read well and enjoyed books, we could learn anything. She was right!

I hated math when I was young. I didn't understand it and I still don't. One day, in homeschool, I was doing geometry and I had just about had enough. I was crying because I was so fed up with it. Nothing made sense and I was frustrated. Mom closed the geometry book and put it away. For a long time, I did zero math. Mom always prioritized our relationship more than she did school. It wasn't worth learning how to plot on a graph if it hurt our relationship with each other.

Above all, Mom prioritized Jesus. Every morning, before school, we would all sit on the couch, memorize scripture, and pray together. She would always say, "I'd rather raise a Billy Graham then an Albert Einstein." Also, Mom said that when we were very young the Lord told her not to worry about Taylor's and my college education; He would provide and make a way for us both. He sure did. With minimal expense and at the age of 18, Taylor completed her college at home, graduating with a bachelor's degree from Thomas Edison State College, and I was blessed with a full-ride scholarship to UNC. I truly believe that the Lord honored my mom's faith and belief.

Nonetheless, school at UNC was hard. There's a very common misconception that athletes have it so much easier than the regular student. No sir, that wasn't the case for me. If anything, I think that certain professors (although not all) make it more difficult for athletes because of the projected stereotype. We had just as much work to complete as every other student, except we had the full-time job of being a D1, college athlete. My freshman year, I also had mandatory study hall multiple times a week. We had weekly check-ins and progress reports with our academic advisor and with assistant coach, Coach Calder. I was held to a high standard along with the standard of perfection that I held for myself. The struggle with perfectionism was real. I about drove myself crazy not only with basketball, but with academics, as well. I was only satisfied if I got an A.

During the season, I would get up early and allow myself at least an hour to do homework before I got ready for a packed day of ball and class. Each semester, my first class was either at 8 or 9 a.m. We had to be done with classes by early afternoon because of our basketball schedule. If I couldn't get my homework done in the morning, I would work during my lunch break or right after supper. I never procrastinated, because I knew if I did, I would never be able to recover from the amount of work. It honestly felt like the homework and studying was never-ending.

I was super pumped because in my first class at UNC, Personal Health, I made an A. I worked so hard for that grade. Mom had never given me and Taylor "grades" growing up. We just completed something until mastery. So, doing school for a grade was a whole new concept for me. That first summer at UNC, I would carry around my textbook and highlighter everywhere I went and read every moment I could. I made flash cards and charts. I used Quizlet for the first time ever and found it to be my best friend. I took my school seriously, just like I did basketball.

Unfortunately, not every class was as successful as the Personal Health class. I'll never forget taking a religion class during my second semester in college. I had been warned not to take any religion classes at Carolina. I had heard they were difficult, stale, and theologically incorrect. Well, I needed a class to fill a certain time slot and as a freshman you don't get as much priority with scheduling classes. You just have to go with whatever class has open spots. So, I thought to myself, "How bad could it really be? After all, it is just archaeology in the New Testament." So, I went with it and boy, was it a doozy. I felt rather confident as I turned in my blue book for my first mid-term in the class. I remember getting my score back the next week and looking down in horror at a 67. I was devastated and embarrassed. The lowest grade I had ever gotten at UNC was an A- and at this rate I was going to end up with a D. Of course, your mind goes to the lowest of places and I started on a downward spiral. I believed my GPA would be ruined, I wouldn't make the Dean's list, everyone would think I was stupid, my coaches would be disappointed in me, and then my world would fall apart. Perhaps if I was this stupid, I would never even graduate! Yes, this is the downward spiral that went through my head. Isn't discouragement one of Satan's most powerful tools? I cried and felt like such a failure. I had studied hard for that midterm just like I had every other class. What went wrong? I had to go to the Teacher's Assistant (TA) and ask where I fell short. Ends up, she was looking for something entirely different and more specific than what had been communicated before the exam. I was pretty upset about it. You best believe that I was much more detailed and borderline overboard on the other midterm and final. I would give her exactly what she wanted! Thankfully, I was able to turn it around and finish with a B+ in religion. I learned a great lesson though; I would never take another religion class at UNC, and I would do a boatload of research before I ever enrolled in another "iffy" class.

I had my share of very difficult courses. There was math. There was statistics. There was economics. With those classes came lots of tears and a desire to quit school altogether. Those classes pushed me to my limits, but thankfully I passed them all and never did as bad as I thought I would. I even made an A- in Stats and Econ, which was a huge win for me. I really knew nothing about either and didn't understand how any of it made sense. However, if you put your head down, make up your mind that you're going to do your best, and use all the resources at your disposal, then you can do it.

I found out, too, that one way to be successful was to be proactive. Staying on top of things you don't know and understand, and going to your TA or professor, is super important. I really hated office hours, but I would make myself go if there was something I couldn't figure out on my own. I thought that going to professors made me look dumb, when in reality, they always appreciated students reaching out.

Thankfully, I learned the ropes as I went through college and gained experiences under my belt. With the Lord's help, hard work, and the prayers of my family, I made multiple Dean's Lists, ACC honor rolls, and graduated with a 3.86 GPA. I was also inducted into Phi Betta Kappa, the nation's oldest college honorary society and one in which less than 1% of all college students qualify. There were a lot of naysayers during my life who said I wouldn't be prepared academically for college and that my parents were doing me a disservice by homeschooling. That couldn't have been further from the truth. To all the homeschoolers out there, you've got this. With hard work, diligence, and God's help, you can accomplish whatever you set your mind to.

# Chapter 19
# My Support System

*And though a man might prevail against one who is alone, two will withstand him — a threefold cord is not quickly broken.*
— Ecclesiastes 4:12

As mentioned, my parents never felt like they could just send me off to college and leave me for four years. So, before I even committed to UNC, they began praying for a place that they could stay or visit often, to be close to me and support me. It would be difficult for my family to afford a house payment in Purlear and a monthly rent in Chapel Hill. Rent is not cheap in that college town! God knew this and provided through a very dear friend of ours. This friend was an answer to our prayers. She bought an apartment in Chapel Hill, three miles from campus, and donated it to my dad's ministry. Because he has a 501c3 ministry and for IRS purposes, I would still have to pay "rent" to CCM (Craig Church Ministries, Inc.), but it would be much less costly than other apartments in the area. Too, women's basketball players receive a "cost of living" check, and I was able to apply that to the rent of the apartment. After our time at UNC, she wanted us to sell the apartment and put the money in the ministry. This was our friend's way of helping our family while supporting CCM at the same time. This apartment was more of a blessing than I can even express.

My family would split time at our home in Purlear and the apartment in Chapel Hill. One of the greatest aspects of having the apartment is that my cat Sarah Mae was able to come live with us. She was my 13-year-old cat who had become a true friend and I couldn't imagine leaving her at home while I was away at college.

She would prove to be my best bud, emotional support, confidant, and companion during my college career.

As a freshman, I was required to stay with my teammates in a dorm, but my sophomore year I was able to move off campus. I moved out of Ram Village and into our apartment. My sister and Mom stayed most of the time in Chapel Hill, while my dad would travel back and forth as much as work and the ministry would allow. College life isn't easy and being a Christian at a liberal college can sometimes be lonely. I was grateful I could come "home" to family and recharge before the next day.

My sister, Taylor, got married September of my sophomore year and moved back to Wilkes County. I missed her so much! We had been together every day of our lives since I was born, and we were very close. Suddenly we went to seeing each other every day to only about once a month. It was hard, as I felt like I had lost my best friend. She used to cook for me at the apartment and help me do my hair for fancy occasions. We would go thrifting on my days off and enjoyed multiple ice coffees at Starbucks. But, just like that, she was gone.

I struggled with her absence, but I was so grateful that I still had my mom. We became best buds. I'm not sure if I would have made it through college had it not been for her support during those years. She was basically my roommate in college and I'm not ashamed to admit it. People can say, "But, oh, you missed out on so much!" Yes, I did and I'm grateful! I missed out on the partying, the temptations, and the homesickness, while I gained so much. I had a companion, chauffeur, cook, listening ear, encourager, and so much more. Too, I gained years of memories with my mom, that only grew our relationship with one another. I'm so thankful for her sacrifice to stay with me and for my dad making the trip down each weekend and allowing Mom to stay in Chapel Hill. My parents only missed one home game at Carmichael Arena and that was the day Taylor was giving birth to my niece, Violet. Taylor and her husband, Zac, would make the trip as often as they could and spend the night with us when they came. I got assigned to the couch, but I didn't mind, as it was worth it for us all to be together. My family's support, love, and prayers are what allowed me to succeed during my time at UNC. I'm forever grateful to them!

My extended family were also huge supporters. My grandparents bought season tickets and rarely missed a home game. They became a staple at Carmichael, along with my Uncle Bubber, Aunt Pam, and cousins. It wasn't unusual for me to have fifteen family members at my games. Other relatives would make the trip to Chapel Hill and come watch me play, as well as friends, fellow church members, and locals from Wilkes County. I was overwhelmed by the support I was shown during my career at UNC. It meant the world to have people cheering me on. I always enjoyed looking up in the stands and seeing familiar faces decked out in their Tar Heel blue and being able to talk with them after the games. Too, I would often have acquaintances, friends, and family at road games. Those are memories for which I am grateful and will never forget.

# Chapter 20

# Overcomer

*But thanks be to God, who gives us the victory
through our Lord Jesus Christ.*
— 1 Corinthians 15:57

One of my fondest memories at UNC would also prove to be one of the earliest. My freshman year, our conditioning test was the mile run. We trained all summer for our test and worked to get in the best shape possible. This meant that many hot, muggy, July mornings were spent out on Hooker Fields, adjacent to Carmichael. We would begin our workout when it was pitch dark and by the time we ended, that July sun would be blazing. I didn't have a car on campus my freshman year, so I would walk up from my dorm at Ram Village in the wee hours of the morning and head to Stallings (our training facility) to heat my stomach with heating pads and do stretches before our conditioning sessions. Oftentimes, I would already be in a complete sweat from the 3/4 mile walk from Ram. Our strength coach, Jason, would lead us through a warm-up and, at my first UNC workout session, I legitimately thought the warm-up was the workout! The "muscle activation" preparation was unbelievable. I was dripping before the session even started. We would jump rope up and down the field, do inchworms, bear crawls, and crab walks. Monster walks with resistance bands would soon follow. There was no doubt we were warmed up by the time we were ready to run.

I've got to say, though, our strength coach, Jason Beaulieu, is the best in the nation. He's amazing and cares so much for his players. He was never too busy to make time for any need or concern. Jason truly wanted to see his players succeed and it was evident in how he cared about us. However, that doesn't mean he wasn't tough. He pushed us to our limit, but we were better for it. We would run 100m, 200m, and 400m runs. Sometimes, our conditioning sessions would be in the afternoon on 95-degree days. It made me mentally tough.

I was still dealing with stomach cramps, and some days it was all I could do to make it through a workout. On some occasions, it was worse than others. Good days I could push through and bad days my trainer would pull me aside and let me take a breath and allow the cramping to pass. It was so discouraging for me. If I couldn't make it through these 400m runs without cramping, how would I ever be able to run a mile straight through? I was in great shape, but it all would just depend how my stomach did on the day of the test. Guards were going to be required to run under a 6:30 mile. Now, that may not seem fast to some, but for me, that was an extreme challenge, even without cramps. I'm not a runner. I'm not built like one and it was a lot to ask for me to make that time ... especially under pressure. Back home in the summer, I once broke the 6:30 mile time at 6:29----but only once!

Our run was scheduled for a September morning at 6:30 a.m. I could hardly sleep the night before. I got up around 4:00, just to get my blood pumping and my body ready. I heated up my water bottle and placed it on my stomach. I did my stretches and ate a light breakfast. And most importantly, I prayed. My family, too, was praying diligently that I would be able to do my best and not cramp.

Our Director of Operations picked up my whole team in a van at Ram Village. It was a little before 6:00 and it was unusually cold for a September morning in Chapel Hill. I'm convinced it must have been in the forties. I don't think any of us said a word on the 10-minute drive. We all knew what loomed ahead. We arrived at an old school track and all the coaching staff, and everyone related to Carolina Women's Basketball, was there. Coach Hatchell had pulled up in her van and turned on her headlights just so we could have enough light to see to warm-up. It was always a rule that we had to match (shorts, shirts, and socks), but we were all freezing in our shorts. However, under the extenuating circumstance of the cold, we got the nod from Coach Calder to wear our jackets, while we ran. I didn't have a jacket, because the freshmen's UNC gear hadn't come in, so I wore an old UNC long-sleeved shirt that I had brought from home. We did a quick warm-up and Coach Hatchell huddled us up and told us the importance of this conditioning test. If you didn't pass the first time, you would run it weekly, until you did. She sent a coach out to each corner of the track so that no one would cut corners. Then we all lined up on the track and waited for Jason's whistle to blow.

My strategy was to stay within distance of Paris Kea, who I knew would easily make her time. If I could just stay close to her, I would make it. I prayed the entire time I ran. I think my eyes were closed the whole run and I just tried to focus on my breathing. By the Lord's goodness the stomach cramps never came. I rounded out the final turn as I heard 6:21, 6:22, 6:23. I kicked it. I was making my time, and nothing could stop me. I ran across the finish line at 6:26. I collapsed to the ground and one of my coaches came to help me up. I did it! I passed my conditioning test, and I couldn't have been happier! I was second on the team behind Paris. Only three of us passed the test, on the first try, and I was the only freshman. I thank the Lord I didn't cramp, and He saw fit to let me make my time. That day will always be one of my favorites as a UNC basketball player. I proved to myself and others that I belonged, and I could compete at that level and under high expectations.

# Chapter 21
# Highs and Lows

*And call upon me in the day of trouble;*
*I will deliver you, and you shall glorify me.*
— Psalm 50:15

It wouldn't be long until I faced my first big bump in the road. During an October pre-season practice, I lunged towards the ball and felt something pop in the middle of my foot. I couldn't walk or put pressure on it. I thought to myself, "This can't be happening." We were less than a month away from the start of the season and Late Night with Roy was happening in only a couple of days. I had always wanted to participate in Late Night in front of a packed crowd at the Dean E. Smith Center. It was the official kick-off for the upcoming season for the men's team, however, the women's basketball team was included, too. Our names were announced, and we were given 15-20 minutes to scrimmage. I was hoping that nothing was seriously wrong with my foot, but deep down I knew there was damage. My trainer scheduled me for an MRI and the news was as I expected. I had a torn ligament in my mid-foot, known as a Lisfranc injury. It would be about 4 weeks before I could start back with basketball-related activity and 6 weeks or more before I could return to games. I would be in a boot with crutches for the upcoming couple of weeks. Late Night with Roy was out of the picture as well as our exhibition games and our first couple of regular season games. Then, we would just have to evaluate things and see how I was progressing. I cried. Yes, that was often my reaction. I was so ready to hit the court as a Tar

Heel for the very first time and this was such a setback. I rehabbed and rehabbed and rehabbed!

As a freshman, it is imperative to be out on the court learning plays and strategies and I was unable to do that. College basketball involves a ton of plays ... a literal book! So that injured players wouldn't just be standing around, they would always be required to go lift during practice. I asked Coach Hatchell and Jason if there was any way I could stay and lift later. I wanted to watch practice and learn the plays even if I wasn't out there on the court. They agreed. So, I would ride on a stationary bike on the sideline while observing practice, then head to the weight room afterward.

A few weeks after my injury, Nicole, my athletic trainer, took me to Carmichael and let me stationary shoot and do some rehab movements. I was discouraged as I couldn't even get up on my toes to shoot, much less jump, cut, and run. The pain was like a sharp, stabbing pain in the middle of my foot. Since those ligaments were torn, getting back to basketball speed would be a challenge. I had worked so hard all summer to get my body ready for the season and just like that, I was at ground zero. Before the injury, I didn't know if I would ever see the light of day on the court, and now, it seemed pretty much hopeless. I had thirteen other teammates vying for playing time and here I was not even able to practice and show what I could do. I questioned, "Lord, you brought me to UNC just to sideline me with an injury?" I didn't understand, but I knew that life isn't easy, and trials come. I could either mope around or attack this recovery with everything I had in me. It was a slow process. I progressed from walking without assistance and without a boot, to climbing stairs, jogging, running and then the final step of making cuts. Planting and cutting were hard, and I felt like my foot would just give out at any moment.

After six weeks, I was finally cleared to dress out and play in my first game against South Alabama. I had missed two exhibition games and three regular season games. I remember seeing my jersey hanging in my locker for the very first time. What a beautiful sight! Across the back, along with the #20, was written the word

CHURCH. It was surreal and I was emotional. Ten years ago, I was sitting in that same locker room as a little camper, hoping, wishing, and dreaming for this day. During the national anthem before the game, the tears overtook me as I saw my family in the stands. God was so good. He brought me this far and I was about to live out my dream.

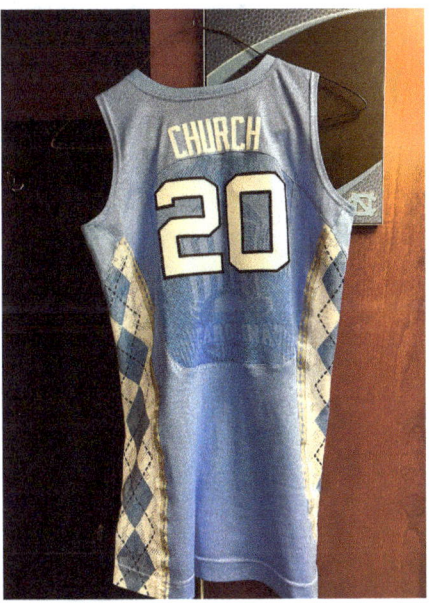

I was sitting on the bench with 6 ½ minutes left in the 2nd quarter when I heard Coach Hatchell call, "Leah!" I hopped up and ran to the scorer's table to get checked in. This was it. I get chills just thinking about that moment. The whistle blew and the announcer said, "Number 20, Leah Church, entering for the Heels." It wasn't but one minute after I subbed into the game that an unforgettable moment took place. I positioned myself in the right corner and watched some action take place on the opposite side. Soon, Paris Kea made a skip pass and found me in the corner. Without hesitation, I shot the ball. As soon as it left my hands, it felt good. I held my follow through and swoosh. My first ever attempt as a Tar Heel was a make! I double pumped my fist as I ran back down the court and then gave the signature Carolina "acknowledge your passer" sign to Paris. I played 10 minutes that game and went 1-1 from the floor. I was on Cloud 9 after the game. However, my foot continued to nag me throughout the season as I would re-tweak it ever so often. I never was 100%, but I worked through it and gave it my best. I was just happy to be out on the court playing basketball at the University of North Carolina!

# Chapter 22

# Standing Alone

*Be strong and courageous. Do not fear or be in dread of them, for it is the Lord your God who goes with you.
He will not leave you or forsake you.*
— Deuteronomy 31:6

There comes a point in your life that you must own your faith and make the decision to stand firm. I had encountered a few of those times in my life. One was at a Carolina camp when I was 12-years-old. I had been ridiculed by a girl that, for some reason, just had it out for me. She would make fun of me and get in my face to provoke and get a reaction out of me. One time on the bus, she finally asked why I didn't go back at her. I responded that I was a Christian. She laughed at me and told me I was weak. I shared Jesus with her and told her I would be praying for her and hoped one day I would see her in heaven. She didn't know how to respond. I think about Lacey quite often and pray for her. That was the first time I had been questioned and made fun of because of my beliefs.

I faced another test of my faith when I started playing at Forest Trail Academy. Some of my teammates asked me why I never cursed, listened to certain music, or engaged in suggestive talk. I explained that as a Christian, I was called to be different and strive to live a holy life. I wasn't perfect by any means, but I tried to honor the Lord in all I did. I kept getting questioned as to the harm, while some of the girls pushed inappropriate images on a cell phone in my face. I closed my eyes tight and resisted. It felt a bit like an interrogation, but after that instance, they respected me and my beliefs.

My faith in Christ, and why I chose to live and believe as I did, would be challenged again at Carolina. It was no longer going to be my parents' faith or my pastor's, but rather MY faith. I was going to need to take ownership. The college culture is not always most glorifying to the Lord, and I had to make the decision of staying true to my beliefs. I had the choice of being lonely and made fun of or going with the crowd and being liked and applauded. It's easy to say that you will stand firm, but the rubber meets the road when you come face-face with that decision. I encountered that choice very early on.

My first week on campus, I was told by several of my teammates that it was required that I go out and party that night. They said that everyone (especially freshmen) had to go. I said, "No, I don't party or drink." They said that there was no need to be shy about it, they wanted me to come, and I would have a good time. I knew there was no way that my coaches "required" me to go out drinking and partying and even if they had, I still wouldn't have gone. It was hard though. I wanted more than anything to be liked and accepted by my teammates and now I felt like they just thought I was "Miss Goody-Two-Shoes." Everyone ended up going out, including my roommates, but I stayed back at the dorm.

Throughout my career, I encountered several occurrences like this. My teammates grew to respect my choice not to drink but encouraged me to go out "even if I didn't want to drink." I personally, however, felt that being in an environment such as a party would be compromising my convictions and could possibly be a stumbling block for others. I spent many nights alone. Some nights I spent studying, while other nights I got up extra shots at the gym. Did I miss hanging out with my teammates and building that comradely? Yeah. I'd be lying if I said that I didn't. But Jesus never said that the Christian walk would be easy, just worth it in the end. Eternity matters much more than fleeting happiness on this earth.

I've also chosen to save myself for marriage. Yes, I know it's counter-cultural. I haven't ever dated or been in a relationship because God has yet to bring anyone into my life. I'm of the belief that I don't have to go searching for the right guy and "test run" multiple guys to see if they are the one. I feel that this oftentimes leads to heartbreak and with each relationship you give a part of yourself away that you can never get back. I desire one day to get married, but until then, I will wait on the Lord and keep trusting Him to direct my steps.

In college, I was looked at as crazy when I said I had never dated or kissed a guy. I have heard it all. "How will you ever meet someone and get married if you don't put yourself out there? You're missing out on so much fun! This is college and you are supposed to have a good time! You mean you've NEVER been out on a date? What's wrong with you?" Don't misunderstand. I desire to someday be in a relationship and be loved and cherished by someone. My family and I have been praying for my husband since I was a little girl, so I will trust and wait on the Lord. Until then, I'm not going to play around with my heart. Just because the culture says to do this or do that, doesn't mean that you should. God honors our efforts to please Him, and we can do this by pursuing purity and holiness. The Bible says in Romans 12:2, "Do not be conformed to this world, but be transformed by the renewal of your mind, that by testing you may discern what is the will of God, what is good and acceptable and perfect." If your life looks crazy to the world, then it probably means you're doing something right. Yes, it would have been easier in the short run to just go with the crowd and have a good time. Trust me, I wanted to be liked and have friends. I didn't want people to talk about me in a negative way and consider me to be some weirdo. Life was lonely in college. But temporary happiness wasn't worth sacrificing my beliefs and convictions. If Jesus can die on a cross for me, then the least I can do is live for Him. Take heart fellow Christian, "… let us not grow weary of doing good, for in due season we will reap, if we do not give up." (Galatians 6:9)

# CHAPTER 23

# THE MOUNTAINTOP

*In his hand are the depths of the earth;
the heights of the mountains are his also.*
— Psalm 95:4

My freshman year, I played about 12 minutes a game and averaged 3.5 points. I was considered a three-point specialist and respected by defenses when I came into the game. I was listed as "shooter" on our opponents' scouting reports. I shot 40.6% from three, my freshman season, which was good for the 3rd best in the entire ACC that year. I contributed to my team by shooting threes, but also by bringing energy whenever I came off the bench. Most people perceived me as "little ol' quiet, meek, Leah," or as my teammates called me "Churchy." But when I stepped on that court, a switch flipped. I am super competitive, and the bottom line is that I want to win ... sometimes getting a little excited and emotional about it! It was not uncommon for me to slap the floor on defense, to get the crowd and our team fired up. Fist pumps and "Let's go!" screams were a frequent occurrence, and the fans grew to love me for it.

College basketball is crazy when it comes to the amount of work and time you're required to put in. It's a job and your payment is your scholarship. In season, a normal day for me looked like this:

7:00 a.m. Wake up at and eat, do devotion and study,

9:00-12:30 p.m. class and eat lunch on the way to get taped and do "treatment"

1:15 p.m. get up extra shots

2:00 p.m. film

2:30-4:30ish practice
4:30-5:30 p.m. weights and food at Carmichael afterwards
5:30 p.m. head back home to shower and do homework.

Sometimes there were tutoring and study hall sessions at night and mixed into our days were academic meetings, extra recovery sessions, office hours, recruiting obligations, group project meetings, community service, etc. Also at Carolina, I was involved in UNC's Leadership Academy and Athletes in Action (a Christian organization). I was chosen by my coaches to be on the SAAC (Student Athlete Advisory Committee) and represent UNC Women's Basketball. This was an honor, as I was able to collaborate and have a say-so regarding issues and concerns on legislation surrounding NCAA sports. Each team at UNC had 1-2 representatives per sport.

It was a non-stop schedule with very little downtime. Each week, we got one day off. Our off-days still consisted of treatment and recovery, getting up shots (optional), and sometimes, community service. All the work and sacrifice were worth it, though, when you ran out of that tunnel and onto the court. I hear it now, the band playing the UNC fight song, a sea of blue with all the fans in Carmichael arena standing, clapping, and cheering. The arena was filled with so much history. Our locker room still had the same door cut-out that Michael Jordan ran through, when men's basketball played at Carmichael. There are tons of banners hanging in the rafters, representing all the NCAA tourney appearances, sweet 16, and final 4 runs, as well as the awesome 1994 national championship banner. There's really no place like Carmichael and every time I took the court, I soaked it all in.

The most memorable game of my career took place on January 21st, 2018. My whole life, I had dreamed of playing in this game, the greatest rivalry in all of sports … Carolina vs. Duke. I was so pumped, and it just felt different. The atmosphere in Chapel Hill was filled with excitement, anticipation, and maybe just a little bit of hate, when Duke came to town. This was my first UNC/Duke game, and I didn't know what to expect. I just knew I was

*Long Shot*                                                                                          111

hyped up, nervous, and excited all at the same time. A couple of teammates and I had a tradition of getting Starbucks before our home games. I remember going and ordering my usual café misto with coconut milk, two pumps of caramel, and extra hot. I was so amped up I could hardly drink it. My teammates were also hyped. All the talk leading up to that game was positive and we talked of how we were going to win and upset the "Dookies." At that time, they were ranked 15th in the nation, and we were unranked. They had a very strong team and a couple of their players are currently on WNBA rosters. We were by far the underdogs. But, when it's Duke/Carolina you can throw rankings and everything else out the door. The rivalry is special, and anything can happen! Before the game, I posted a picture on my Instagram of me, as an 8-year-old, wearing a Carolina headband, pointing to a sign that said, "Beat Duke." Things had come full circle and it was my time to live it out!

Carmichael was packed out on that Sunday afternoon at 2:30, with close to 5,000 fans in attendance. The energy was electric, and I still get cold chills thinking about it! Duke played a 2-3 zone to start the game, so I was subbed in very early to try and bust open the zone and spread the court. I hit my first couple of shots, and it was surreal. I had come in the game averaging 3.1 points and already passed my career high of 8 points, by halftime. Unfortunately, we fell behind fast in the second quarter and found ourselves

down by 19 points. Kudos to my team, though, because we never stopped believing and fighting.

In the second half, we slowly chipped away, and the crowd got into it. I started slapping the floor on defense and the bench would slap the floor, too. Soon, we were all in unison, slapping the floor and yelling, "Defense!" We meant business and this game was not out of reach. Paris Kea was having the game of her life and Jamie Cherry, our point guard, was dishing out the rock like crazy. It was the perfect storm, and we were making our comeback. I played almost the entire game, having only averaged 11 minutes a game, up to that point. Thank goodness, my adrenaline kicked in, otherwise I would probably have been gassed. Getting tired and winded wasn't an option!

The end of the game was epic and will be a classic, forever. Holt McKeithan, of the Daily Tar Heel newspaper, detailed the legendary ending in his article, *Take me to Church*... (You've got to love the play on the name).

"Down three points to No. 15 Duke with four seconds left in regulation, North Carolina women's basketball head coach Sylvia Hatchell drew up a play. Who did Hatchell trust to shoot with the game on the line? It wasn't Paris Kea, a pre-season All-ACC Team pick who finished the game with 36 points and five made threes. It wasn't Jamie Cherry, the senior leader known for her clutch late-game shooting. It was Leah Church, a first-year averaging 3.1 points a game. "We were trying to do a flare-type screen and a cross-court pass for Leah to shoot it," Hatchell said. "But it wasn't there." Since Church was so closely guarded, Taylor Koenen instead threw the ball into Kea, who drained the triple with one second left on the clock to send the game to overtime. Though the play didn't pan out as designed, the fact that Hatchell picked Church, who had never scored more than eight points in one game, speaks volumes about the confidence the head coach has in her. Perhaps that confidence comes from Church's 48-percent shooting from three on the season. Or perhaps it comes from something else. "Look up on your phone, put her name in:

Leah Church. YouTube it, and it'll come up," Hatchell commanded. "She makes 33 threes in one minute." Hatchell was off by one, but the feat is no less impressive. Inside the Wilkes Family YMCA in the fall of 2016, Church set a world record by hitting 32 threes in one minute. She broke the previous record of 27, and, as the video's description notes, ending up making 55 before missing. So, despite limited in-game experience — Church came in averaging less than nine minutes a game — she was not afraid to let it fly. The Purlear, N.C., native had a career-high 19 points and shot 5-11 from 3-point range, "I believe in my shot because I've put in the time and put up the shots," Church said. "I'm confident and I've just got to give credit to Jamie and Paris because they have confidence in me ... and that means a lot, especially as a freshman for them to trust me." According to Kea, however, Church's value goes beyond her shooting prowess. "She brings a lot of passion to the game," Kea said. "You can see it all over her face. She just brings so much energy ... she gets us started." Her energy was on full display when she jumpstarted a listless North Carolina offense in the second quarter. In a nearly five-minute stretch that started in the first quarter, UNC did not score. Church broke that drought. The 5-foot-8 guard was fearless in her drives to the basket. After being blocked on a drive the previous possession, she took it right back to the hoop and drew a foul. Later in the second quarter, when UNC was down 19, she went on a personal 5-2 run. She drained a deep two-pointer from the right baseline, then followed it up on the next possession with a swish from three. Immediately after, Church, whose play is consistent with the basketball maxim "Shoot to get hot; shoot to stay hot," pulled up for a heat-check three that airballed. But despite that miss, her seven second-quarter points sparked North Carolina's comeback. Church continued to energize the Tar Heel offense. In the third quarter, she hit a clutch three from the corner to bring the Tar Heels within one. Then, in overtime, she connected on two threes that helped seal the 92-86 victory for the Tar Heels. Even after the best game of her career, Church remained humble. "First off I've got thank my Lord and savior Jesus Christ because to be in this position, it's a dream come true for me to have the opportunity," she said. "My teammates, they found me and they looked for me, and thankfully some of them went in today."

The Lord truly did exceedingly and abundantly more than I could ask or think. (Ephesians 3:20-21) Really though, could it have been scripted any better? I posted my career high against Duke, with decisive 3-pointers in overtime to seal the win and then was called up to the press conference? Little girls lined up for my autograph and to have their pictures taken with me. I was humbled. I had so many people texting me and congratulating me on social media. I had someone say that they watched the ending at a restaurant in New York, since the game had been nationally televised on ESPN2. My Uncle Bubber had been traveling from Texas and couldn't make it to the game. He told me he watched the game on his phone through the ESPN app and was sitting there crying in the airport. He couldn't believe his eyes. Uncle Bubber said everyone was looking at him like he was crazy and even gathered around to see what was happening. I was overwhelmed by the support.

As I walked back to my car with my parents and sister, I broke down sobbing, in the parking lot. I posted this tweet, along with my favorite picture ever taken during my UNC career. The caption read, "All His Glory! I broke down crying in the parking lot after this game. It hit me … all the hours of work, the sacrifices, the doubters, the tears, the times I wanted to quit…. Yet, a dream I held onto of being in the spot I was today. I was overwhelmed. God is good, y'all." So, there it is, the story of my favorite memory at UNC. UNC vs Duke + God = anything is possible!

At the end of the season's UNC Women's basketball athletic banquet, I was presented two awards. The first was for the top 3-point percentage on the team and, second, was for the most inspirational player. Both of those awards meant so much to me, as I prided myself not only in my shooting ability but also my character and attitude. To have that recognized by my coaches meant a lot to me, as I closed the chapter on my freshman season as a basketball player at the University of North Carolina.

# Chapter 24

# Repping My Country and My Faith

*Let each of you look not only to his own interests,
but also to the interests of others.*
— Philippians 2:4

The following summer, I was chosen to represent the USA at the FISU (International University Sports Federation) World University games in São Paulo, Brazil. These games are similar to the Pan-American games. It was an honor to have the opportunity to play basketball in Brazil and represent my country. The head coach of the team, Jane Albright, had previous connections with Coach Hatchell and said she needed a shooter and my name came up. She also heard that I was a strong Christian and felt like this trip would be perfect for me. We would be representing Athletes in Action, a Christian organization headquartered in Ohio. Girls from all over the nation would make up the team and Susan Yow, the sister of NC State's legendary coach, Kay Yow, would be our assistant coach. The NCAA teams represented on our team were: Oregon State, Arizona State, Iowa, Montana State, Nevada, Washington State, Elon, Xavier, and of course, North Carolina.

I was somewhat hesitant about going because I would miss summer school, summer practices, and workouts. I was afraid that missing the summer might negatively impact my playing time and contributions for next season at UNC. However, I prayed about it and the Lord gave me peace and told me to "Go." I was a little nervous traveling out of the country, without my family, and on a trip without anyone I knew. I was also fearful of getting homesick.

We would be gone for almost 2 weeks. My mom cried when she told me goodbye at the airport, and I teared up. It would be the longest time that we had ever been apart, and I knew it was hard on her to let her "little girl" go out of the country.

The first three days would be spent in Xenia, Ohio for training camp and the remainder of the time would be in São Paulo for the FISU games. Packing a two-week supply of basketball clothes as well as snacks (essential items) in a single suitcase is tough and proved to be about the most difficult part of the trip. At the Athletes in Action headquarters, men's and women's basketball were going to be represented along with volleyball. There were a lot of athletes and coaches on the campus, and it was buzzing.

I got settled into my dorm and saw that my roommate was Megan Gustafson. Little did I know that she led all of NCAA Division I in scoring, was a first team all-American, and the Big 10 Player of the Year, for Iowa. All I knew was that she was one of the kindest, most humble, and genuine people I had ever met. Having her as a roommate in Ohio was a good start to the trip. We had meetings and training sessions as well as devotion times. It was incredible because even though we were there for basketball and to train to win a gold medal, you could feel the presence of the Lord surrounding the place and people. We were presented with our USA gear upon arrival (shirts, sweatsuits, jerseys, backpacks, etc.) and would practice once a day, with the option of getting up extra shots in the afternoon. Several of us went to Xenia's local YMCA with the director of our trip, Bonnie Durrett, to lift weights and do some strength training. Oftentimes it was just me, Hannah Stewart (Iowa), and Megan (Iowa). Of course, afterwards we would have to stop on main street to get some local coffee. That proved to be a necessary outing.

The most special part of this trip was that Jesus was the focal point. We were in it to win and would end up playing teams from Brazil, Chile, Mexico, and Uruguay, but we would also have 2-3 minutes after each game to share a testimony with them. I had always hoped and prayed to use basketball as a platform to share the Lord, and this would be the perfect opportunity. I volunteered to share after one game and started preparing what I would say.

We finished the preparation in Ohio and would soon be headed to São Paulo, Brazil. As I mentioned before, I had been to Brazil once as a little girl, so I was excited to be visiting for the second time. We had experienced a wonderful time of discipleship in Ohio, and I had started bonding with a lot of my teammates and people on the trip. It was incredible to be surrounded by so many people who loved not only basketball, but Jesus!

The accommodations in Brazil were great. The USA and every other team stayed under one roof. There were over 1500 athletes and 12 countries represented. It was an amazing atmosphere. We ate with people from different countries, traveled by bus with others, and drew people from all over by hosting devotions and outreaches in the hotel. We had multiple translators and it was awesome to see how the Lord could overcome the language barriers and move in a great way.

I have always stood firm in my faith and been outspoken about it, but this trip took me to a whole other dimension of being bold in sharing Jesus. I led in one of the small groups during these devotion times and it was a bit intimidating. I was having to use a translator and didn't have a clue about the lives of the other competitors. It's amazing when you are obedient to the Lord, he gives you the courage and help you need. This was just one of the times that the Lord's presence was so very evident, on this trip.

The day we arrived in Brazil, the opening ceremonies took place at the Brazilian Paralympic Center. All the teams carried their country's flag and were introduced to the beat of festive music. I honestly felt like it was the mini-Olympics. The president of the FISU games spoke, as well as other notable people from Brazil. It was a neat opportunity to be exposed to other cultures and ethnic groups. The people in Brazil were so kind and welcoming!

We didn't start our games until later in the week, so we had a couple of days to do other things. On our first full day, we partnered with Samaritan's Feet and passed out shoes to disadvantaged children in a very poor area of Brazil. It broke my heart to see the conditions these kids lived in, but their happiness and joy were incredible. They were so positive and kind. I had the privilege of washing some of the kids' feet and sharing about how Jesus washed the feet of others. Through this act, we were able to share the Gospel. After we finished washing their feet, we would hand them a new pair of shoes. It was one of the most wonderful experiences and changed my perspective on life, itself. I had so much to be grateful for and realized that the only thing that truly matters is Jesus and sharing him with others. Everything else is so trivial and unimportant. I tend to get caught up in myself and everything pertaining to me, but the only things that matter are the eternal souls of people. I'm grateful that through basketball I was able to have this opportunity that changed my life.

The next day, we visited local shops and the marketplace. There were so many souvenirs and unique items (food, trinkets, and other goodies). It was a highlight of the trip. While out and about, several of us got a sandwich and split it three-ways. It was rather tasty, even though I have no idea what kind of meat was on it. Some memories just make you smile!

We only had one practice before our games and had to be aware of the differing international rules. The three-point line was further back (by about 2 feet), the lane was wider, the line-up for free throws was different, and there were a few other adjustments. We cruised through our first couple of games, as our team was stacked. We had a lot of talent, size, athleticism, and shooting ability, and it was difficult for the international teams to match up with us.

After each game, we would circle up and share a quick testimony, pray, and get a picture with the other team. Those opportunities were even better than the time we spent on the court. Each team was so grateful for us taking the time to speak to them and to show we cared. Showing Jesus doesn't have to be a huge production, it can literally be holding hands in a circle after a game and saying, "Jesus loves you and so do we." We handed out AIA bracelets with a scripture verse on them and spoke about what the verses meant to us. It was a sweet time.

I shared my testimony after our game with Mexico. I spoke about my surgery, the Lord's grace through it, and how He got me back to the basketball court. I then shared about the miracle of getting to play at UNC. I encouraged them to trust Jesus with their life and how He wanted a relationship with them. There have been few times that I have felt God's presence like I did in that moment. I cried when girls from the other team started crying. After I prayed at the end of my testimony, I found out that one of the girls had just lost her father. She had debated on foregoing the games but was grateful she decided to play so that she could hear this message. I was so humbled and heartbroken by her story. I pray that she found her hope in Christ, as it's truly all we have.

On our off-day, we visited Rio de Janeiro. It was beautiful! We toured Christ the Redeemer and Copacabana Beach. My favorite part was haggling for a good deal, with the vendors on the side of the road. I still have the knock-off pair of polo sunglasses I bought for practically nothing. They're my favorite sunglasses and still going strong!

On the basketball front, we cruised through group play and faced Chile in the semi-finals. It was neat because the games were live-streamed, so everyone back home could watch. We won and advanced to the championship where we would face Brazil, one of the toughest teams in the tournament. Interestingly, there were some delays which pushed our championship game way back. We were already at the gym that day ready to play and couldn't head back to the hotel, since it was about an hour's drive. We all were starving and knew we would have to find something to eat. Our team got Ubers to McDonald's and enjoyed a "pre-game" meal that included McChickens, Big Macs, nuggets, fries, and milk shakes. I've always been a stickler when it comes to diet and nutrition before games, but at this point I didn't care and didn't have a choice. Hey, maybe, it worked for us. Later that evening, we ended up winning the gold medal by beating Brazil 59-42. We were champions and it felt so good!

I consider the Brazil trip to be one of the greatest experiences of my life. I developed lifelong relationships and friendships, my faith was strengthened, my perspective changed, and the trip allowed me to represent my country and become a gold medalist. I'm forever thankful for that opportunity and it will be something I will always remember.

# Chapter 25
# Disappointments

*Better is open rebuke than hidden love.*
— Proverbs 27:5

Life as a student-athlete is a full-time commitment, but days off were filled with lots of Chapel Hill flare. You could oftentimes find me at Al's Burger Shack, eating the best cheeseburger and fries around or at YoPo, a frozen yogurt place on historic Franklin Street. Mom and I made frequent trips to South Point Mall and Lumina theatre for a movie. Sometimes we went thrifting at some local shops in Durham and Chapel Hill. The summer heat in Chapel Hill can be brutal, so we would hang out at our apartment pool and sip on some kombuchas to keep cool. A lot of good memories were made on those days and are some of my fondest. It really helped to break up what can sometimes be a monotonous, grueling schedule.

I never took for granted the times of impromptu shooting sessions I'd have at Carmichael. Walking into the gym with my own passcode and having 24/7 access, with the court to myself, was like a little slice of heaven to a basketball lover. I was living out my dream and no one would ever be able to take away the fact that I played basketball at the University of North Carolina. Carolina blue had always run through my blood and it always would. I was ready to get my sophomore season started and was excited for what was ahead.

Just because you are living out your dream doesn't mean you won't face difficulties. As a Christian, you are targeted even more as Satan wants to do all he can to beat you down. My freshman year, I had experienced some pressure and bullying, but it intensified my sophomore year. One girl on my team especially had it out for me. Every practice, she would stir things up and constantly blame and humiliate me. I took it silently for a long time, until one day in practice, I finally went back at her and told her to stop doing things just to make me look bad. She was literally making my life miserable, and I couldn't keep going on like that. I think a lot of times, we think that Christians are supposed to be a doormat and let others walk all over us. I disagree. "Like a muddied spring or a polluted fountain is a righteous man who gives way before the wicked." (Proverbs 25:26) I had never done anything to her, but she just didn't like me and wanted to see me fail. Of course, my coaches were somewhat surprised that I even opened my mouth and said anything. After practice, they took me and my teammate aside and sat down with us to hash out our "issues." I couldn't believe what she said next. She told the coaches not to be fooled by me that I actually cursed on the bench and in the locker room and was not as good of a person as I portrayed. She continued to slander my name and was trying to defame my character. They were all such lies. Anyone who knows me knows that I have never said a curse word. Ever. It's not who I am. I couldn't believe that she had said all these blatant lies to the coaches just to get me into trouble. The truth remained that this teammate had one of the crudest mouths on the entire team, so it was ironic that she was saying that cursing makes you a bad person. Thankfully my coaches knew my character and did not believe her. Still, it hurt me so bad, and I was very upset about it.

    I didn't understand how or why someone could dislike me so much for trying to do the right thing. But as I look through the Bible, there are multiple instances of Christians being hated and attacked for standing on their beliefs. Luke 6:22 says, "Blessed are you when people hate you and when they exclude you and revile you and spurn your name as evil, on account of the Son of Man!" When I read this, I realized it was an honor to be attacked on account of my faith in Christ and my character. If you are going through a similar situation of being bullied or mistreated, I encourage you to keep doing the right thing and living the right way. Don't be afraid to confront those who are responsible for the wrongdoing. Over time, the relationship between the two of us somewhat improved. It was never great, but it was manageable.

I know that it isn't easy to keep doing the hard things and the right things. With basketball, too, I always prided myself in not getting into trouble. I tried to always be on time, make sure I had on the right color undershirt, do well academically, attend every class, and hit the benchmarks that were set each game (boxing out your man a certain percentage of the time, not giving up a specified number of rebounds, etc.). If you violated the rebounding rules, as a game starter, you would lose your starting position for one game. For the other violations, you would have a 6 a.m. scheduled time with our strength coach, Jason (which one wanted to avoid at all costs).

My freshman year, one of our seniors (who was also a starter) didn't hit her benchmark during a game, so that meant she couldn't start the next one. Which game would that be? Duke, in historic Cameron Indoor Stadium. I knew since I was one of the few others that hit my benchmark for rebounding, I would be next in line to get the start. I couldn't believe it! I would get the chance to start a game versus Duke, in Cameron. I was ecstatic! Granted, I was sad for my teammate, but rules were rules and we all had been held to this standard the entire year. I called and told my mom about getting to start the Duke game. I knew she would be so happy and excited!

The next day, I heard that the coaches had a meeting and said they felt since it was this player's final game at Duke, she needed another chance. They were going to hold a vote for the team and if we all said yes, then she would start. Everyone, including me, voted yes. I was glad for her, but deep down, I was hurt. It seemed something like this never failed to happen and there were no rewards in doing good or doing the right thing. I didn't go out and party so I wouldn't miss curfew before a game. Others did. I would get good grades and study in my free time. Others wouldn't. I would get up extra shots every time I could and others rarely did. I would be respectful to my coaches and give it all I had and play through minor discomforts and pain. Others wouldn't. Yet, it sometimes felt like I didn't get the nod with playing time, even if I had played well the game before. It was something I had to work through during my time at UNC, and I knew that the Lord would honor my efforts, even if I couldn't see it at the time. It was hard not to give up and say, "What's the point?" But I would always go back to Colossians 3:23: "Whatever you do, work heartily, as for the Lord and not for men." It was my job to do the very best I could in everything I did and whatever happened after that was in God's hands. I couldn't bear to have any regrets when my time at Carolina was done. Regrets like, "I should have gone harder or studied more or showed up earlier," were not an option. No, I would give it my all. If I was rewarded in playing time and great performances, then wonderful. If not, then hopefully God would be glorified in it all and one day, I would see the fruits of my labor.

# Chapter 26

# Unforgettable!

*And he awoke and rebuked the wind and said to the sea,
'Peace! Be still!' And the wind ceased, and there was a great calm.*
— Mark 4:39-40

Thankfully, God doesn't let you stay in the valleys forever and he allows you to get to a mountain top, every now and then. I had two such experiences my sophomore year and boy, were they high points!

Not everyone gets the chance to host the #1 team in the nation on your home court. The benefits? It draws a huge crowd. Who doesn't want to see the legendary and defending national champs, Notre Dame (coached by Muffet McGraw), led by All-American, Brianna Turner, or Notre Dame's all-time 3-point record holder, Marina Mabrey, or ACC female Athlete of the Year, Arike Ogunbowale? Up to this point, the Tar Heels had experienced an average season. We were 12-9 overall, and 3-4 in the ACC. However, we weren't intimidated by the thoughts of Notre Dame. We had prepared all week with a sense of confidence and Coach Hatchell had talked about making this game our "Wow-moment!" No one was thinking we could take down the defending National Champs, except us. We strategized and game-planned, but honestly, we knew it would still take a miracle for us to pull it off.

I was so excited because all my family was going to be at Carmichael to watch this game, along with almost 5000 fans. I had over 20 family members that had made the trek from Wilkes to support me. The atmosphere was crazy. It was almost as hyped as the Duke game, my freshman year. Notre Dame also had a significant number of fans, as they have one of the best fan bases in women's basketball. My freshman year we had played at Notre Dame, gotten beat by 32 points, and their biggest post player fell and landed on my head, smashing it into the ground. To make matters worse, I was pinned there for five seconds. So, I thought to myself that it can't get any worse than that!

The day of the big game, I grabbed a quick bite to eat with my parents, sister, and her husband, Zac, at Ye Old Waffle, on Franklin Street. It was the location of most of our pregame meals during my sophomore year. I told them that I really thought something great could happen that day. It just felt special, and our mindset and focus were different. I got excited about every game, but I was absolutely stoked about this one. I knew their team was big and athletic and I may not get to play a lot. But I also knew Notre Dame liked to play a zone, which gave me a chance at getting some playing time.

The entire game was back and forth. Notre Dame's largest lead of the game came in the first half when they were up six. There were 8 lead changes and 3 ties. I played a few minutes in the first half and got one shot attempt. I missed. We went into half-time down by 2 points. When an underdog is playing a top team, it's one thing for it to be close at half, but you know to expect the better team to pull away in the second. We were happy to be down by only two but knew we would have to keep playing well and with energy to hang in there.

Our crowd was amazing, and the energy was electric in Carmichael. We even got up by 10 at one point in the 4th quarter. But, like #1 teams do, Notre Dame came roaring back. Coach Hatchell chose to play me quite a bit in the fourth quarter because of Notre Dame's zone defense. I was able to spread the court so that Paris Kea (who had an amazing game and ended with 30 points) could get to the basket. They had to respect me as a shooter in the corner of the court. I had only gotten one shot attempt but was glad I could at least be a decoy to help my team. The game was all tied up at 71-71 with 1:25 left. It was beginning to sink in that we really could knock off the number one team. We had possession of the ball and it was a crucial point in the game. I ran the baseline a couple of times, and we shifted the defense. Then, suddenly, their zone-defense lost me. The ball was coming to me (in what seemed like slow motion), on a skip pass from the top of the key. I caught it in the corner and launched it with no hesitation. I didn't have time to think that I had only shot once all game, that we were playing the top team in the nation, there was only 1 minute left, or that 5,000 fans were anxiously holding their breaths. No, I just trusted the thousands upon thousands of shots I had taken in an empty gym, in preparation for this moment. The ball carried and I followed through. Swish! It was pure! That ended up being the game winner and we never relinquished the lead. What an amazing feeling to celebrate a win like that one! It was a true team-effort and a "Wow-moment!" that I'll never forget. I came out of the locker room to a line of young girls and people waiting for my autograph and picture. It is something I never took for granted. It was humbling and I was so appreciative for the support. On SportsCenter that night, our upset was covered over and over again, and my 3-pointer was the top highlight of the game. People from all over were texting me to say that they had seen me on SportsCenter. It was one of my favorite memories at UNC and one that I get chills every time I relive.

My Uncle Bubber, who is also my pastor and one of my biggest supporters, wrote this on his blog, the day before we played Notre Dame ... so great!

> *"Does prayer work? Does it work in your life? When is the last time you prayed for something and it actually happened? As you are thinking, let's go even deeper. If what you prayed for actually happened, how do you know for sure it was your prayer that caused it to happen? Was it your prayer or someone else's?*
>
> *Those are tough questions to sort through. Certainly they are in my own mind sometimes. The truth is...on this side of glory, it's hard to tell for SURE about the specific answers to the questions I've asked. But, let me say this...I do believe prayer works, because*

I've seen it work in my own life. Can I say for SURE it was my prayers that did it...well...

I told you last week that "Sports Is Life." I saw that come to fruition this weekend again! Let me go to last Saturday. I told you that from time to time I might find a few minutes to go out and shoot some hoops. I did this Saturday evening. I knew I needed to get a little exercise and get some "steps" in...so, out the door I go. My "go to" is basketball, of course. Just shoot and run from corner to corner and do the "around the world" routine. So, I started. It was cold. About 30 degrees and it was about 5 o'clock. I knew I didn't have long. There was stuff to do for the evening. Nonetheless, I was nailing shot after shot.

As I was shooting, I started thinking about my niece, Leah Church, who plays for the Lady TarHeels. They were playing Notre Dame the next day. Notre Dame just happened to be the #1 Women's Team in the country. They had lost just one game...to powerhouse UCONN. It was going to be a tall task. The Heels have had an up and down year... They had an 11-9 record and were 2-4 in the difficult ACC.

Now let me say this...I don't think the Lord is that interested in the outcome of ball games. I just really don't. In the scheme of important things in life and eternity...whether it's basketball, football, baseball...you name it... It's just not an "eternal proposition" in most cases. Yet, I do believe He wants us to pray for our loved ones to do their best and for safety and things such as that. So, as I moved from shot to shot, I breathed a prayer for Leah and I said, "Lord, just help her and the team do their best. And Lord, give Leah 7 shots." Why did I pray for 7 shots? That's a big number for any player coming off the bench (which Leah usually does). But, I thought, "You have not because you ask not." And I knew if she got up 7 shots, she'd hit 4 or 5 of them because she's an amazing shooter! In fact, I asked several people to pray with me for 7 shots. And several said they would.

As I continued to shoot and pile up some "steps," it hit me... "You are really nailing these shots today." So, I had this crazy idea! I thought, "Video what I call 'around the world' and send it to Leah." Just do the best you can and send it. So, I set up my phone on a bucket and shot this video... (listen what I say at the end)...

*Nutty, huh! But, hey...I hit 9 of 11 after missing the first shot! So, give me some credit! Ha! I'm 50 years old folks!* But, I wanted Leah to know I was thinking about her and praying for her. So, I sent it to her and she texted back, "that made my day..." And so, "mission accomplished."

The family and I loaded up and headed to Chapel Hill on Sunday. Yes, I said, "Sunday." I've never done that. In 14 years of ministry, I've never missed a Sunday except for vacation or a mission trip. But, I believe I needed the break and family needed me to take the break and the truth is… I wanted to go! Yes, I could have sent my family without me and preached. I've done that before. But, the church is in excellent hands when I'm gone, so we went with total confidence and peace.

Have you heard what happened? Is it even possible the Heels could beat the #1 team in the country? Well, first of all I want to tell you what happened with Leah. She didn't get 7 shots off. She only got off two. In fact, in the first half, she got up her first shot and missed and pretty quickly was taken out for the game. I thought, "Oh no...this is going to be tough." But, as the game went on and the second half came...she got back in the game. The Heels were playing well. A guard for the team, Paris Kea, was on fire. She ended up with 30 points and 10 assists. Amazing! But, in order for the Heels to pull off the massive upset, something needed to happen.

With 1:25 left in the game the ball comes to Leah in the corner. The entire arena was standing. I literally held my breath. I froze and it felt that time stopped. She caught the ball (would she shoot it or pass it back...would I shoot it...I don't know...oh my...this is the number one team in the country...she's not shot a single other shot in the game...would she have the nerve to take this shot...this is such a risk...such a gamble...but, she can shoot the lights out...she can make it), she set her feet and released the ball...it's in the air...

The sound in the arena was strange...it was amazingly loud up to that moment...but, it was like a collective "breath-holding" moment for everyone. The ball splashes through the net and it sounded like a sonic-boom in the arena! Watch…

*Did you watch the bench stand up when the ball was passed to her? They knew it was in! Paris Kea…the leading scorer in the game is the one who passed her the ball and she's already backing up going down court the other way. She knew it was in too!*

*Pam happened to video the shot from our seats behind the basket! Needless to say, all the family went nuts: Me, Pam, Clara, Andrew, Katy, Josh, Charlotte, Evelyn, Kandace and Clark!*

*My mom and dad were in their seats to our right and below us. They have season tickets and of course, Kim and Craig, Taylor and Zac were in their familiar spots on the front row down below them. Not to mention that Craig's family (dad and step-mom, step brother) was in the arena as well. Needless to say, there were plenty of #20 Leah Church fans in Carmichael Arena!*

*Now, why do I tell you all of this?*

*Honestly, I really believe with all of my heart that the Lord heard the prayers of our family and those close to Leah. Did God answer my specific prayer? Obviously not! I asked for 7 shots, but she only got 2. But, it only took 1 to answer my prayer! Do you see! The Lord can answer our prayers even when it's not exactly what we ask. He has a plan that's so much better than ours. In fact, Leah said it best on Facebook!*

*Does prayer work? Ask Leah Church. This is a woman who knows more about prayer and the hard work of it than anyone I know.*

*Let me tell you something…prayer works. James says, "The prayer of a righteous person has great power as it is working" (James 5:16). That picture above you is a prime example of that. So, pray! Pray when it seems impossible! Pray when you miss the first shot! Keep going…Keep living! Look for the next chance and keep praying! It's worth it! Even when it's just going 1 for 2, and you asked for 7!"----Uncle Bubber*

After we upset Notre Dame, we went on to beat undefeated NC State at Reynolds Coliseum, in Raleigh. They were ranked in the top ten, so it was thrilling for us to get the win. Following those

*Long Shot*

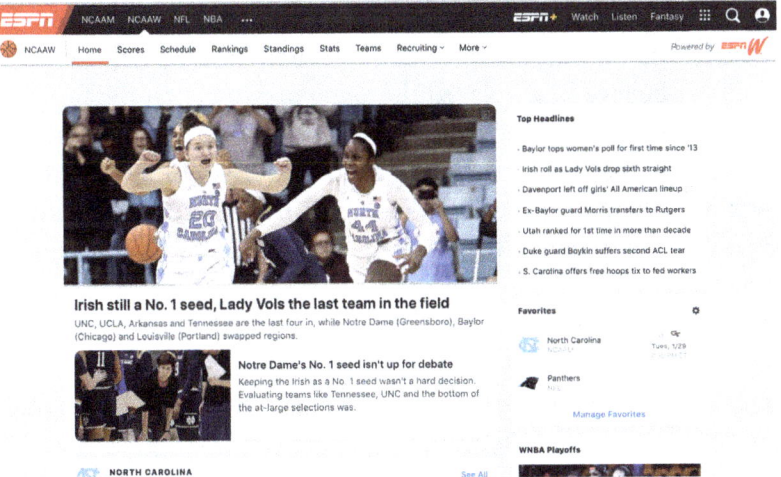

two victories, there was talk of us having the opportunity to make the NCAA tournament, that year. Since we had an average start to the season, this was huge to even be in the discussion. We really needed to pick up a win or two in the ACC tournament to secure our spot and feel confident, come selection Monday.

I loved the ACC tournament which was held in Greensboro, NC. I grew up attending the women's ACC tournament and always longed for the chance to play in it. One year for Christmas, I got an all-session ticket package to see every game. Since then, I was enamored. I used to sit in the stands with my family imagining myself playing in a game, instead of just catching t-shirts in the stands and eating Dippin' Dots. Although, that was fun, too! My parents would always buy me a tournament t-shirt that highlighted all the teams and I treasured each one.

Since one of our starters was ineligible to start, I got the nod to start our first ACC tourney game vs Georgia Tech. Georgia Tech started out in a zone press, so I got behind the defense and set myself up on the three-point line. My teammates found me, and I scored the first 9 points and went 3-3, from three. I tripled my scoring average in just 4 minutes. It was one of those games that my shot just felt pure! I ended up with a career high, 20 points on 6-8 from three-point shooting, while playing 37 minutes. I was the "Hardees Player of the Game," so the TV commentators for Fox Sports South recapped and highlighted my performance. I couldn't believe I had played the game of my life on the big stage of the ACC tournament.

I was so blessed to have big moments at big times, whether it was my freshman year vs Duke, or against #1 Notre dame, or at the ACC tournament. My best performances usually came at some crucial times. It was during these times that my dream of playing for the Tar Heels was so fulfilling and I couldn't believe that it was real life. I had young girls look up to me and want to be just like me. One little girl came up to me wanting a picture and autograph. She had her hair up in a bun and was wearing a blue headband, like mine. Her family said she tried to look just like me. Who could ask for more? Moments like that kept me going through the more challenging times. It was special to receive letters that said, "You inspire me to go for my dreams" or "Thank you for being such a good role model in how you carry yourself." That made it all worth it!

We ended up making the NCAA tournament and faced California in the first round in Waco, Texas. We were the #8 seed. Unfortunately, just a few days before we were to leave, I woke up sick with a sore throat and achiness. Everyone felt sure it was just a cold, but I went to the doctor just to make sure. I was sent back to my apartment before our afternoon practice and my trainer called and told me that I had tested positive for the flu. We were leaving in two days and my coaches didn't feel comfortable with me traveling with the team. So, they booked me a separate fight to travel with my parents. I was disappointed; this was the NCAA tournament and I had worked so hard to get to this point. I was going to miss out on the travel experience, plus I felt like a dog!

I made it to Waco, met up with my team, and practiced that afternoon. I was so very sick but was not going to let it stop me from playing in the NCAA tourney! I drank an over-abundance of Pineapple Coconut Body Armor just to stay hydrated and did my best to eat and keep food down. I went 2-2 from three with 6 points and played 17 minutes, against California. But unfortunately, we lost. My career shooting percentage in the NCAA tournament is 100%, because that was the only opportunity I got to play in it! But I'm grateful for that time and happy I got to experience making the NCAA tournament as a Division I athlete!

My sophomore season was over, and I had highs and lows. It was sometimes frustrating, as I knew I was capable of scoring and contributing (as against Georgia Tech and in the ACC Tournament) and had hoped for more chances to play to my full potential. In college (and in life) things aren't always fair and so, you make the best of what you get and maximize the opportunities that are given to you. I felt like I did that and had done the best I could with the hand I had been dealt. I was thankful to be playing at that level and representing UNC. I had come a long way from just hoping to be subbed in for technical foul free throws.

I loved the tradition and history that came with Carolina, not to mention being Jordan brand sponsored. The gear and shoes were awesome! We would receive about 8-10 pairs of shoes each season and a pair of Jordan retros. Gear days were the best and my closet is still stocked full of that beautiful Carolina blue. There's really nothing better. I loved that several of my coaches were Christians and supported me and the stands I took for my faith. Prayer was welcomed. Cursing wasn't allowed on the court. Standards were high. The Carolina way was respected. Carolina was a cherished place and one that came with the highest distinction. Little did I know that a change was about to take place and much of what I knew and loved about Carolina would soon be taken away.

# Chapter 27
# The Battle Line

*With him is an arm of flesh, but with us is the Lord our God, to help us and to fight our battles.*
— 2 Chronicles 32:8

The off-season, following my sophomore, year was a crazy one. Some unfortunate events took place which forced Coach Hatchell to resign from her coaching position at UNC. The Hall of Famer amassed over 1,000 wins over the course of her coaching career and spent 33 seasons leading the Tar Heels. Coach Hatchell is a legend and will go down as one of the all-time winningest coaches in history. The entire coaching staff was swept clean and big changes were made. It was hard to see the coach that gave me my chance at UNC leave. From the time I was very young, she was one of the reasons that I had loved Carolina. When you thought of UNC women's basketball, you automatically thought of Coach Hatchell and one thing you could never doubt is how much she loved the Tar Heels and the university.

It's so sad how things went down and to this day I don't understand why things happened the way they did. After 33 years of coaching, why did the change have to take place during my career? I only had two years left to finish playing at my dream school. Nevertheless, it happened, and things were shaken in my life. I knew it was a rarity and I was blessed to have had supportive, Christian coaches, especially in an environment such as Division I women's basketball. I was praying and hoping that the Tar Heel legacy would be carried on by a former player who bled Carolina blue and understood the tradition and honor of wearing that wonderful jersey.

The athletic department went in a different direction, and I knew it was going to be challenging for me. I had been given this opportunity at UNC, as an act of God and due to Coach Hatchell's belief in me. So, I would have to work to prove myself and show that I belonged on the team. I could do the work, but my faith would not allow me to fit into the mold that was now expected. I, once again, was faced with the decision to compromise who I was and what I believed was right. Approval became based on expectations … go out with recruits and show them the "fun" of college life, be a "loud" voice in the locker room and forceful in my opinions and accept the foul language (now allowed and modeled) in practice. Choosing not to abide by these actions, I was perceived as weak and inadequate. I became an easy target.

My confidence took a hit. I am the first to admit that I am not the quickest player on the court and sometimes got beat off the dribble … many people do. Unfortunately, I was singled out and belittled for each infraction. On many occasions in film, I would hear the comment of my inadequacy on defense and the need for my team to "help Leah in her matchups." Although I was not the fastest, I tried to make up on defense by sacrificing my body and taking charges. So, even though I wasn't a starter, I led my team in charges taken. However, another day, practice was stopped, and my teammates looked on as I was cursed at for not shooting a shot. I would have chalked it up to just coaching style had I not been the only one called out for such things. It was demeaning and I felt as if I was alone on some distant island. There was no connection, no relationship, no approachability. However, since scholarships are renewed on a year-by-year basis, I was grateful to have my scholarship renewed and position maintained for another year.

Nonetheless, that summer was a difficult one, to say the least. Not only had basketball become a challenge and a heavy weight, but I was also taking an economics class that was super difficult. The combination led me to a very dark place. There were many times I would come back to the apartment after class or practice and I would just lie on my bed and cry. I felt like that was all I could do. There were times I didn't think I could keep doing what I was doing, but each time the Lord gave me the strength and stamina to keep going. It wasn't my time to be done, so God sustained me through it all. At this point, Psalm 73:26 summed up my life, "My flesh and my heart may fail, but God is the strength of my heart and my portion forever."

I was physically tired and exhausted. The 6 a.m. lifts and conditioning, skill workouts, and practice were draining. Because of camps in Carmichael, we would often practice in Woolen gymnasium, in the summer. Remember, Woolen was not air conditioned. Let's just say those practices were character builders. We were pushed beyond our limits. I remember running stadiums at Kenan during preseason. We hopped and ran up over 3000 steps that day and my calves locked up. I couldn't walk that evening and Mom had to help me down the steps to get in my apartment. My calves were like bricks and I couldn't get them to release at all. I went to my trainer for therapy, but they weren't improving, and I was sent to the doctor. I had overdone it and my muscles were in spasms. Since I could barely walk, I missed one day of practice and did rehab. My calves were locked up for about 3-4 days. My body felt like it had been through the wringer not to mention the mental stress of basketball, new coaching, and my classes that summer.

Thankfully, we were able to come home for about two weeks in August, before fall semester classes. I needed a break and time with family. It's always been interesting in my life how the Lord knows exactly when you need to get out of the valley and stand on a mountain top, for a little while. He knows just when to give a reprieve and encourage His children. One night when I was home, my sister and brother-in-law were over for a cookout. We were sitting outside on the driveway, and I was shooting around on my basketball goal. I told my mom to record me because I was going to try and make two backwards shots from beyond the three-point line. I had made one before but never two, consecutively. I gave my sister 3 balls and told her to pass the next ball to me once I hit the previous one. I spent about 30 minutes chasing misses and balls down my driveway, and I finally hit two in a row. On cue, my sister passed me the third ball and I hit it! I was happy, but honestly, I thought it was no big deal. I wasn't even going to post it on Instagram, but my sis and Mom told me it was neat and impressive and I should post it.

It wasn't long before SportsCenter shared my video across all its platforms, followed by Bleacher Report, Sports Illustrated, espnW, WNBA, Fox News, and more. My original Twitter video on my account had over 1 million views. Several local news stations interviewed me and broadcasted my trick shot video. One morning, after I posted it, my Aunt Pam texted me and said that her aunt had seen me on the Today Show. Sure enough, a bit later, people were sending the me the video of my shots shown on the Today Show and even on the national Fox News. Friends in Ohio, Florida, and other places said they had seen it. I was amazed. What started out as nothing, the Lord took and made it into something. It was such an encouragement to me, and I was grateful that God, once again, saw fit to take my video and use it. Not everybody gets the opportunity to go viral once in their lifetime, much less a couple of times. All the glory to God! If you'd like to see the video, just for the fun of it, google "Leah Church backwards shots."

The following season was a battle for me and one of the lowest points in my basketball career. My biggest fear was happening before my eyes ... basketball was no longer fun. The constant replays of my shortcomings and failures during film and prep work were embarrassing and humiliating. I was used to being shown my mistakes by the previous coaching staff, but once it was addressed, they moved on. I dreaded scouting for a team we had already played, because I knew my defensive assignment and miscues would be over-analyzed and highlighted. I honestly felt like a complete failure.

Due to foul trouble, matchups, or injured teammates, I would sometimes play the fifth most minutes on the team and more than even some starters. After our regular practice, our starters were able to get massages during the season, while the rest of us had extra, intense skill sessions and weights. Even though I played more minutes than a starter, I would be put in the group doing the extra work. My strength coach inquired about this and suggested that I get to rest and recover, but was told, "Oh, I'm sure Leah doesn't mind and wants the extra work." I was told that I was just "in between" groups and there wasn't a perfect group for me to be in. One of my injured teammates, who didn't play at all, even asked permission to give me her massage slot. I appreciate that she cared.

It didn't matter how much I played or how well I played, nothing changed. There was one instance the day after we had lost to Duke that I was pushed to a breaking point. During that game, I had played almost as many minutes as a starter. The following day, we had our normal film breakdown, an over 2-hour practice, and then the "non-starters" had a 45-minute, on-court workout session, followed by lifting. Other than the starters, I had been the only other player to play significant minutes, yet I was assigned to the routine of the non-starters. I was exhausted, felt worthless, and believed my performance didn't matter. Our extra session included full-court zig zag drills, continuous one-on-one, and defensive and other intense drills. If we messed up at all, we had to start over and couldn't quit until we got it right. I wasn't the only one who felt like giving up. It wasn't uncommon for others to leave the court, with tears in their eyes.

That day on my way to Stallings for an ice bath, I had what I would consider a full out mental breakdown. It was the beginning of February and freezing cold, yet I was dripping in sweat from practice and the extra workout. I called my mom, huddled outside in a nook where no one could see me, and told her I didn't think I could do it anymore. The injustice and unfairness were blatant, and I felt hated and belittled. For the first time in my entire life, I uttered words I thought I would never say, "I hate basketball." It was gut-wrenching for me to admit that to myself. I was sobbing, uncontrollably, as I came to grips with the circumstances.

That season, I had played through a rather severe shoulder injury which I sustained at the beginning of December. The MRI showed trauma to my shoulder: an AC sprain (which meant shoulder separation as well as fluid and bone bruise), and damage to my bicep tendon. The pain was intense during every practice and game. If I got bumped or hit, sharp shooting pain would overtake me, and I would reinjure it, repeatedly. We tried taping and padding my shoulder, but nothing seemed to help. To make matters worse, it was my right shoulder, my shooting arm. I was at my wits end with everything related to basketball. But I'm not a quitter and we still had a whole month of the season left, so I would finish it out to the best of my ability.

I had never really struggled with anxiety and the feeling of self-worth. Now, however, I couldn't escape it. When you are a DI college athlete, the sport is your life and the people in your sport are those with whom you spend 99% of your time. I felt so alone, and I no longer had basketball to fall back on. It wasn't enough. I turned to my family for prayers. God seemed distant during that time and Satan was trying to beat me down.

I made it to our final game of the ACC tournament, and we knew we weren't going to get a birth in the NCAA tournament that year. As it ended up, Covid would hit and prevent the tournament from being played at all. Deep down, I knew after our loss to Wake Forest in the ACC tournament, I had worn a UNC jersey for the last time. I was bawling my eyes out when I came out of the locker room and saw my family waiting for me. They knew, too. I even stuck my white, UNC game-worn jersey in my bag. I knew they wouldn't be needing it again. Even though I felt I wouldn't be playing at UNC my senior season, it took three months for me to get peace and come to grips with that decision. Those months proved to be some of the most difficult of my life.

The bright point, of that season of time, was my niece's birth. It goes without saying how close I am to my sister and how much I wanted to be there for the birth of my niece. She was due on January 23, smack-dab in the middle of my season. I knew it would probably be impossible for me to be there for her birth because I could be playing an away game, traveling, or have a game at

Carmichael. Well, on December 30th, we got a call from Taylor at 12:15 a.m., telling us her water broke and Violet was on her way (3 ½ weeks early). Much to my disappointment, I had a home game at 2:00 that day, so I knew I would probably miss Violet's birth. I was a nervous wreck and always had my phone beside me. As soon as our game ended, I checked my phone and expected to see that she had been born. Instead, the text revealed Taylor was at 8 cm. I immediately got on the road to make the 2-hour trip to the hospital, hoping I could get there in time. I had a bag already packed and skipped post-game meal and recovery. Literally, as soon as I walked in the door, Tay started pushing and Violet arrived 30 minutes later, at 7:25 p.m. It truly was a miracle that I made it in time and could be at the birth! Too, since we were on Christmas break, I didn't have classes the following day and that day just "happened" to be our one off-day. I say "happened" because nothing just happens by chance. I was able to spend a day with my precious Violet and was beyond thankful to have experienced the birth of my beautiful niece.

# Chapter 28
# The Time has Come

*I have fought the good fight, I have finished the race,
I have kept the faith.*
— 2 Timothy 4:7

We didn't make the NCAA tournament, so we were allowed to go home for spring break. Little did we know that, due to COVID, we wouldn't be returning for the rest of the year. I hated that a pandemic spread throughout the world, but honestly it was an answer to prayer for me, as I was able to be home. I needed that time to think, pray, and be around family and away from basketball. We were all still required to be on zoom calls with the team and coaches, do workouts, and report our results. Although I began thinking more on the idea of forgoing my senior year of basketball, the thought sickened me. How could I give up something that I loved so much? Carolina was my dream, right? How could it be God's will for me to leave early? Why did it have to turn out this way? Why did a coaching change have to take place during MY career? Could I live without basketball? What would others say and think? Would I regret it? The questions just kept spinning around in my head. I was scared.

Because of COVID, UNC was allowing students to take up to nine credit hours each summer session, rather than the usual six. If I took the max in the summer, I could graduate in December, rather than next May. If I wasn't playing basketball, there was nothing to keep me at Carolina for another semester. Even though I hadn't fully decided to forego basketball, I did decide to go ahead and enroll in 6 classes for the summer. Although it was going to be a difficult load, I had to take these classes if there was any way I was going to graduate early. In a normal semester, with basketball, I would only take 4 classes (12 hours). So, six classes over the span of just two months was going to be a stretch.

During this time, while up in the air about basketball and taking these classes to graduate early, I had a full-out panic attack. It hit me hard and laid me flat on my back! I had just found out that my three required classes in the first session of summer school were going to run through the second session, as well. That meant that for over a month, I would be on zoom for class from about 8-2:30 each day (with 15 minutes between classes), have homework for six classes, daily group project meetings, and discussions. My classes included Astronomy, an Astronomy lab, an online internship, Statistics, Data, Sales, and Political Thought. I was overwhelmed and I broke. It was an attack directly from the enemy. I laid in my bed for two days straight. I cried. I didn't eat. I wouldn't talk to anyone. I didn't even get up for those two days. I just felt stuck. I didn't think there was any way I would ever be happy again. If I gave up basketball, I would be heartbroken. I had never known life without basketball. If I didn't give up basketball and went back to play, I knew I would be miserable and eventually must compromise my beliefs and who I was.

I thought I would never survive the summer with the whole course load. I hated school and I hated the classes I was going to have to take. I would never graduate. Where was God in all this? Why did He work such a miracle of getting me to UNC just to let it end in this way? I loved Carolina! I just didn't know how I could go on. For those two days, I didn't move and felt like the weight of the world was sitting on my chest. I couldn't breathe and it was all just darkness. Spiritual warfare was rampant, and Mom would tell me, "This is an attack from Satan, and you can't just give up. You have to fight." She told me, "This is not you, Leah." I knew she was right, but I just couldn't shake it. I had been through so many difficult times and hardships. I had been determined and resilient. I had been strong! But not now. I was like a wilted flower.

I don't know what turned around. I'm sure it was my family praying for me. Honestly, I was upset at God for letting things turn out like they did. But as I thought and talked to my parents, I realized that we can't always know and understand the will of God and why things happen like they do. Looking back, I see how God spared me. If I had played my senior year, I would have been faced with so much pressure to compromise and turn my back on my faith. I would never have made it and God gave me a way out. He used COVID in my life to give me time at home to pray and evaluate my options. He also orchestrated the COVID pandemic in such a way that UNC allowed me to take more credit hours to graduate early.

I made the decision in June 2020 to go to Chapel Hill and tell my coach I was not coming back to play. It was the toughest decision of my life, but after three months the Lord gave me peace. I told my mom, "I can't believe I'm giving up a year of basketball at Carolina." She told me, "It's not the same Carolina you fell in love with as a little girl." And she was right. I had made it and played for my dream school, Carolina, but the UNC of present, was no longer my dream. I had fulfilled everything I had wanted, and God had done more for me in that time than I could have ever imagined. I marked my name in the history books of Carolina Women's Basketball and nothing or no one could ever take that from me.

I cleaned out my locker and took one last look at the banner hanging over Carmichael… "Playing at Carolina is an honor, winning at Carolina is a tradition." This was the same banner I stared at as a 7-year-old camper and now, here I was at 21 years old, having lived it out. I could honestly say that I lived my dream. Even if I had stayed that final year, there really was nothing more that could have been added to my legacy and career at UNC. God was through with me at Carolina, and I had to trust His plan and timing.

I may never know why things ended up like they did. Sometimes we just have to exhibit faith. Do I wish I could have played out my final year? Of course! But I was blessed. I was going to be an alumna of the University of North Carolina in December 2020. Having played basketball on a full scholarship for the Tar Heels, I would leave with more memories than I could ask (Duke, Notre Dame, Georgia Tech, etc.) … moments that will be with me for a lifetime. And hopefully, all those young girls who looked up to me would have the courage to pursue their dreams and see evidence that, with hard work and the Lord, dreams really do come true!

My mom did a great blog post on her homeschool Facebook page (Homeschool Reflections), regarding my decision to leave UNC. Her analogy of Moses and the Israelites is so fitting. It reads: "Will They Know When it is Time to Go?

On June 24th, our daughter, Leah, met with her basketball coach at Carolina, and told her she was graduating early and would not be finishing her senior year, with the team. If you know us or follow our family, you perhaps can understand what a difficult and gut-wrenching decision this was for Leah. Literally her whole life has been spent playing basketball and working toward the goal of playing at Carolina. Her desire was attained, and the goal accomplished, when she was recruited and offered a full scholarship, three years ago. So, what happened to compel her to finish basketball and school early?

In answering that question, I am reminded of Moses. The Israelites were living in Egypt after moving there during a famine. God would send Moses to lead them out and see them to the Promised Land. Why did they have to leave? The Israelites were in bondage to Pharaoh and the Egyptians, but also the Lord knew if they stayed, they would lose their identity and their distinction as the people of God. Egypt had become a foreign land whose principles and commands did not line up with the Lord's. It was time to go.

No doubt, leaving Egypt was difficult for the Israelites. It was a hard existence, there, but it was what they knew. It was the familiar. But, at some point I am sure they realized in their spirit that the end had come. The opportunities were before them that would set them free. They could trust God to get them home.

The circumstances surrounding Leah's decision is nothing short of amazing. The Lord has had to work overtime to orchestrate her departure. Covid-19 has afforded her the opportunity to take 16 credit hours this summer, which is an over-load that allows her to be set up to graduate a semester early (in December), she will be able to do remote classes (from home) this fall, and she would still have a year of eligibility should see decide to play basketball somewhere else and pursue a graduate degree. It would have taken an act-of-God (maybe a world-wide virus) to shut down Carolina and to remove Leah from college and the setting in which she found herself. I feel in my heart that just as God sent the plagues to set His children free, He has done the same for Leah. I had prayed for removal and the Lord answered that prayer. Although Covid-19 has been tragic for so many people, He can even use bad things for good.

Even though the signs seemed clear that Leah was to finish basketball and college early, it was often hard to be sure. Like Moses, there were times that she asked if it was really time to go. The Promised Land of home seemed so far away and getting there would not be easy. There was still much to do…people to inform, plans to make, schedules to adjust, preparations to be made, doubts to overcome, questions to answer, the familiar to leave, and the unknown to face. But faith had to win out over fear.

There will be times in our children's lives when they know the Lord has brought them to a situation or place. However, there is nothing in scripture that says that they will always remain in that setting, position, or circumstance. Will they have ears to hear, "It's time to go?" Sometimes, even when a place becomes the wrong fit, they will have to make sure that they see it as such and get out. As parents, we need to be teaching our children to identify red flags, unhealthy environments, and toxic people. We live in a world engrossed by all of these and must never become comfortable with darkness. There are instances that our children will need to "stick it out" and finish strong and there are other circumstances when they have finished the race and it's time to head back. Talk about danger signs and the need to sometimes flee, the importance of remaining true to their identity in Christ and honoring the Lord's word. Discuss that sometimes the right thing takes courage and overcoming fear. Fortunately, Jesus is always there…in the dark tunnel, in the water when we are drowning, when we feel we are suffocating, and all the rest of the not-so-great times.

Equip your children with skills to get where they are going, fortitude to blossom where they are, and the insight to know when they need to leave. I can rather emphatically tell you; they will need them.

> *"Then I said to you, 'Do not be in dread or afraid of them. The Lord your God who goes before you will himself fight for you, just as he did for you in Egypt before your eyes, and in the wilderness, where you have seen how the Lord your God carried you, as a man carries his son, all the way that you went until you came to this place.'" (Deuteronomy 1:29-31)*

# Afterward

# Long Shot

*But he said, 'What is impossible with man is possible with God.'*
— Luke 18:27

    It's been two years since I made the decision to walk away from basketball at UNC. I'm now a 2020 alumna of the University of North Carolina with a degree in Exercise and Sport Science (with a concentration in Sport Administration) and a minor in Coaching. After a lot of hard work and God's help, I graduated with a 3.86 GPA and with highest distinction. I wrote this book a year ago about 10 months after I chose to walk away from UNC. It took me that long to process the emotions of how things ended at Carolina. I know in my heart that the only choice I had was to forgo that final year and I truly believe that it was God's plan for my life. Yet, it was still one of the hardest decisions I have ever had to make. I cried many tears while writing this book and reliving the memories. To be honest, I lost my love of basketball that final year at UNC. I never thought that could possibly happen. You've read my story and you know how much I adored and loved basketball. It was my life and my motivation. I even had another year of eligibility to play college basketball and pursue my master's degree, but I never felt God leading me in that direction.

    I struggled to even talk about basketball for an entire year, much less pick up a ball. It has taken time, but my passion and love for the game is returning. I don't think that my whole life was filled with basketball just to have a few people and experiences take away my desire for the game. I've always felt that basketball would be a part of my life and that is proving to be true to this day.

I had the opportunity to assist coaching at a local high school this past season and am currently training and doing shooting skill sessions and basketball camps. However, I think the most incredible thing is how God has opened many doors for me to share my testimony and journey. I was approached by The Gospel Coalition and asked if I would be willing to share my story and talk about why I left UNC. They wanted to encourage others to stand firm in their faith and titled the article "Choosing God over Basketball." They released the article during March Madness. After the article was published, Franklin Graham shared it on his Facebook and Twitter pages to an audience of over 12 million. Mr. Graham wrote, "I like people who've got guts for Jesus, people who will stand boldly like Daniel. Leah Church is one of those people. She had always dreamed about playing basketball for UNC, but gave it up to stand for her biblical beliefs. Leah said, "I knew I wasn't going to be able to compromise and go against biblical principles. I decided, in light of eternity, that basketball wasn't worth it." She chose God over basketball. You made the right choice Leah, and God will bless you for it! Leah said she kept coming back to James 1:12: "Blessed is the man who remains steadfast under trial, for when he has stood the test he will receive the crown of life, which God has promised to those who love Him." After that, CBN News, with over 1 million followers, also shared my story. Since then, the Lord has given me several opportunities to go and share my testimony. I count it a privilege to use the platform that God has given me through basketball to tell others about Him.

I have been able to talk about the Lord's faithfulness and goodness in allowing me to achieve my lifelong dream of playing at UNC and I share that the only thing that matters in this life is whether you know Jesus as your Savior. It doesn't matter if I played at Carolina, hold the world record for 3's in a minute, graduated with honors, or went viral on social media. There is no peace and happiness in anything apart from knowing Him. I truly believe that God allowed me to accomplish my dream at UNC and has given me success in basketball to give me a platform to share about Jesus and bring him glory.

I'm thankful for my story. Against all odds, I am a nobody from Wilkes County, who the Lord saw fit to allow to achieve a lifelong dream to play basketball at the University of North Carolina. Not only did I get to be on the team and play, but God also gave me many highlights and memories. I'm grateful for the ups and the downs as they have made me the person I am today. I feel as though I am stronger and more determined than I would have ever been without them. I'm thankful for the trials in college, as they tested my faith and strengthened my dependence on God. I'm thankful for my family and for the sacrifices they made on my behalf and all the prayers and encouragement.

I'm thankful for my mom encouraging me to write this book and share my experiences and thoughts. Writing is not my favorite pastime or something in which I am especially good, so I put it

off for a while. I had received a book from my church for graduation, entitled, "Don't Waste Your Life," by John Piper. It was then that the Lord spoke to me and told me that I had all these experiences and an incredible testimony of His faithfulness that shouldn't stay bottled up inside of me. That is when I decided to write down my story.

I hope and pray, despite obstacles or naysayers, you will find encouragement to pursue your dreams.

I pray that you will see the faithfulness of the Lord through my story and His miracle-working power.

I hope that you will see how far hard work and determination and trusting a big God can take you.

I hope that you will be encouraged to stand firm in your faith and always choose Jesus over everything else.

I hope that you will be inspired that even in the difficulties, God is still there, and His plans are bigger and better.

Most importantly, I pray that if you don't know Jesus as your Lord and Savior, you will call on him, today. He waits with open arms, ready to receive anyone who comes. "For God so loved the world, that he gave his only Son, that whoever believes in him should not perish but have eternal life." (John 3:16) I'm blessed and grateful and I thank YOU for reading my story....

a dream ... a long shot.

# The Last Chapter ... For Now

*I press on toward the goal for the prize
of the upward call of God in Christ Jesus.*
— Philippians 3:14

(In between finishing my book and the release date, the Lord added another chapter. Thus, here is the second, "Afterward"…)

It was the evening of October 18, 2022 and I was sitting in my living room voicing my worries to my mom. The last two years of my life had involved me playing the "waiting game" and as I wondered what was next for my life, I was becoming discouraged. I told my mom, "It's hard, because all I want to do is compete. I find the most fulfillment when I'm competing and it's just too bad at my age, there are very few ways to do that." That must of jogged her memory, because mom replied, "Did you ever text that coach back?" She was referring to Coach Campbell, the head coach at Union University, who had texted me three weeks prior, inquiring about my final year of eligibility.

Let's rewind a bit. On September 1, Naomi, my former teammate at UNC, (who was now a grad transfer at Union) had texted me. We went back and forth with small talk and then she mentioned that the coaches wanted to talk to me. I never responded. You may be thinking, "Wow, Leah, that's kind of rude." Yes, I would agree. However, I mentally couldn't even think about the possibility of playing basketball again. I had hung up my jersey and I was retired. Several colleges had contacted me, since leaving Carolina, with offers of a full scholarship. But, if we are being totally honest, the thoughts of picking up a basketball actually scared me and I had absolutely zero desire in finishing out my extra year of eligibility. Plus, I put the address of Union University into Google Maps and realized it was over an 8 hour drive from my home. So, without the desire to play basketball and the additional drawback of being that far away from home and my family, I totally disregarded the idea and didn't respond to Naomi. That is when Coach Campbell texted me, a few weeks later, asking if I'd be willing to talk. I ignored him for three weeks.

So, we're back to Oct. 18 and mom's question. I told her, "No, I haven't responded to him," and like most moms, she told me that if only out of courtesy, I should text him back. Mom also added that it would probably be good for me to hear him out since you never want to completely close off potential relationships. It took everything in me, but I responded the next day and said although I wasn't very interested in playing my final year, I'd be happy to talk. Coach Campbell called me later that afternoon. He cut straight to the chase and told me that he had read my article (in which I gave my testimony in the *Gospel Coalition*) and felt like I would be a great fit at Union. Coach Campbell proceeded to tell me that they were implementing a new style of play ... a full court press on every possession. Because of the fast pace and intensity, he felt he would need more bodies and as a shooter, he felt the team would be getting more possessions, because of the press. This, in turn, meant more three-point attempts for a shooter like me. He added that we have the same beliefs and the same mission for God. Coach Campbell then said he had a full-scholarship for me. Considering we were three weeks away from the start of the season, I assumed he was talking about me coming next year or at the beginning of the next semester, in December. I asked him this and he told me, "No. I'm talking about you playing this season and you being on campus within the next week." I proceeded to tell Coach Campbell that I hadn't touched a basketball in over 2 ½ years and he responded simply, "I know."

I was somewhat flabbergasted and my brain was trying to process things. This took place on a Wednesday and he told me that he wanted me to come for a visit the next day, because if I came to Union I would have to make a decision and be enrolled by Friday. I don't really know what got into me and why I didn't shut down immediately and say, "No, thank you," but I told him to give me 15 minutes to mention this to my parents. I walked into my living room where my mom and dad were standing and told my mom, "We need to go to Jackson, Tennessee, tonight." Mom responded, "Give me 30 minutes and I'll be ready." And in 30 minutes, mom and I were on the road heading to Jackson, TN and I had absolutely no idea why. I just felt like I had to go.

I thought that maybe I had to go visit just so I would never wonder "what-if?" I was truly just trying to rationalize it all. We drove down and spent the night and visited for a couple of hours on Thursday. As I talked to Coach Campbell, he explained that he was just being obedient to God, because he felt like the Lord wanted him to offer me this opportunity. He kept highlighting the importance of the full-court press and how he felt I could help them on the court, but also by who I am as a person. I was upfront and honest and told him, I just didn't know if I could come to Union. Basketball scared me and leaving my family did, too. He told me to take 24 hrs. and pray about it and give him an answer by Friday night. Mom and I started the long drive home and I was so stressed. Through tears, I told mom, "I don't even know why I'm even considering this. It's all crazy."

I knew I had to let Coach Campbell know the next day and I was so torn. I didn't want to miss out on something if it was what God wanted me to do, but the thoughts of being 8 hours away from my family for six months and moving somewhere completely new, while starting a master's degree, was terrifying. Not to mention, I was being asked to play basketball again … a game that, to put it bluntly, I hated. I had continued to work out over the years but I was now 24 years old and hadn't played or shot basketball in 2 years and 8 months. I knew if I went, I was setting myself up for failure and that fear was almost debilitating. Mom told me, "Don't let fear be the reason you don't go." We were about 4 hours into our drive and I was struggling. I asked God to please give me clarity and a sign or something so I would know what to do. It was at that very moment, a memory popped in my head, something I hadn't thought of since the moment it happened. Coincidental? I think not.

I remembered back to September 23rd when I spoke at the *Salt and Light* conference to approximately 400 people in Charlotte, NC. I gave my testimony of being at UNC and the importance of standing for your beliefs. After the conference, I was out in the lobby getting ready to leave when a lady sought me out and came up to me. She told me how much she appreciated what I said and how good it was to see a young person living for Jesus and then she told me , "I have a word from the Lord for you." She said she had no idea what it meant, but she knew it was for me. Then she said these words, "Full-court press." Obviously, having no idea what it really meant for me, I just smiled and said thank you and then I said something to the effect, "Well, we should all have the same intensity for Jesus as a full-court press." And then I walked off and never thought of it again. Until that moment, in the car, when I asked God for a sign. It was some of the first words out of Coach Campbell's mouth during that phone call and what he had been emphasizing the entire time. I teared up. It was at that very moment, I knew without a doubt, I would be playing basketball for Union University, that season.

It's April, 2023, and I've been back home from Jackson, for a month. I've had some time to reflect and think about my time at Union. We won a conference championship and I was able to cut down a net for the first time in my career. We were 27-4 and finished the regular season ranked #9 in the nation. I was able to play on a team where relationships were prioritized and the priority was more than just basketball. I was able to pursue my master's in Christian Studies and although I may not know exactly why God called me to Union, I know, without a shadow of a doubt, I was supposed to be there. Maybe a big reason was simply to act in obedience to the Lord.

Was it easy? No. Basketball-wise, I could tell I had been retired for almost 3 years and it was a challenge to learn the approximately 100 plays and learn to shoot from a three-point line that was now a foot further back from when I played at UNC. I also had rough patches where I was very homesick and discouraged. However, I was able to grow as a person and in my walk with Jesus. When it's just you, on your own, you learn a lot about yourself and are forced to rely a whole lot on the Lord. Through these last three years, I learned that God is always orchestrating your story. I waited over two years for God to bring me something, but nothing ever came … until Union. Some would say, "It was out of the blue." His timing can seem late, but God doesn't go by our time frame. I learned to trust His timing and His direction and to always be ready to walk in obedience.

When I thought of a storybook ending for my basketball career at Union, I thought of a Final Four, an MVP caliber season, or something of that nature. None of that happened. But, when I walked off the court for the final time I realized it was never about that. I was crying and my heart felt like it was breaking, I was devastated it was all over. And then it hit me. Coming back to play allowed me to say four words I thought I'd never say again. Basketball, I love you. I never thought I would have another chapter to this book. Thank you, Lord, for rewriting my ending.

*And we know that for those who love God all things work together for good, for those who are called according to his purpose.*
— Romans 8:28

www.ingramcontent.com/pod-product-compliance
Lightning Source LLC
Chambersburg PA
CBHW050639160426
43194CB00010B/1736